# CHOOSING
# HELP

# PRAISE FOR *CHOOSING HELP*

"Grounded in cutting-edge science and brought to life through deeply human stories, this book offers practical tools for navigating the most common—and often most difficult—reasons people avoid getting help. Whether you're a concerned friend, family member, or a clinician, *Choosing Help* is a must-have resource for effectively guiding others toward the help they need, with empathy, skill, and hope."

—SUDIE BACK, PhD, Director of Drug Abuse Research Training, Medical University of South Carolina

"*Choosing Help* provides concrete, real-life strategies and small steps, to help your loved one say yes to life-changing mental health treatment."

—BOBBI CONNER, producer and host of the Health Focus radio series & podcast

"Friends, parents, teachers, counselors, doctors, and other health providers, especially those who are not familiar with cognitive behavior therapy, will find this book educational and useful. Even experienced therapists will enjoy the examples and benefit from the reminders. I enjoyed and enthusiastically recommend the book."

—BOB DRAKE, MD, PhD, Professor of Clinical Psychiatry, Columbia University

"At times it can feel incredibly daunting to talk to someone about getting help. This book provides practical techniques and easy to understand examples that not only build confidence to initiate that conversation, but to help get your loved one, co-worker, or patient into the treatment they need."

—LISHAM ASHRAFIOUN, PhD, Associate Professor of Psychiatry, University of Rochester Medical Center

"As a clinician and researcher, I see the same barrier over and over: people want help, but anxiety, stigma, and logistics win. This program targets that barrier directly with practical, stepwise strategies and clear measurement. Treatments only work when people get to session one. This gets them there."

—NIK ALLAN, PhD, Assistant Professor,
    Department of Psychiatry and Behavioral
    Health, The Ohio State University

"*Choosing Help*'s thoughtful structure—pairing relatable stories with practical, evidence-informed strategies—makes it an invaluable tool for families, healthcare professionals and students learning to build trust and foster meaningful conversations. It's a gentle guide with a powerful impact."

—TERESA KELECHI, PhD, Dean of Research in the College
    of Nursing, Medical University of South Carolina

"We are on the verge of a great opportunity in mental health. At a time when the Suicide Hotline was rolled out and when young people's mental health fluency is at an all-time high, we need thought leaders to emerge and help us all capitalize on this opportunity. One has, and her name is Tracy Stecker. Dr. Stecker has produced a readable and highly useful book on seeking mental health help. A highly recommended read from a world's authority on the topic."

—THOMAS JOINER, PhD, Director, FSU Psychology Clinic

"In Choosing Help, Dr. Tracy Stecker breathes compassion into the challenging landscape of supporting loved ones who are struggling with their mental health. The mix of storytelling and concrete strategies set this book apart as a beacon of hope and healing while navigating how best to support those we love."

—JENNIFER M. GÓMEZ, PhD, Associate Professor
    of Social Work at Boston University

# CHOOSING
# HELP

## YOUR FIRST STEP TOWARDS
## BETTER MENTAL HEALTH

## TRACY STECKER, Phd

### Foreword by Charles W. Hoge, MD

Hatherleigh Press, Ltd.

62545 State Highway 10, Hobart, NY 13788, USA

hatherleighpress.com

# CHOOSING HELP

Text Copyright © 2025 Tracy Stecker, PhD

Library of Congress Cataloging-in-Publication Data is available.

ISBN: 978-1-961293-46-5

Cover Design by Carolyn Kasper

Printed in the United States

The authorized representative in the EU for
product safety and compliance is

Catarina Astrom, Blästorpsvägen 14, 276 35 Borrby,
Sweden. info@hatherleighpress.com

10 9 8 7 6 5 4 3 2 1

*To my Dad.*
*To anyone who feels alone.*
*Light and love.*

# CONTENTS

# FOREWORD
# BY CHARLES W. HOGE, MD

**C**HOOSING HELP IS a gem of a book, a roadmap for how to communicate with someone resistant to seeking help. Mental health problems touch all of us in one way or another, either personally, or among our immediate family members, friends, co-workers, or classmates. We all need the skills imparted in this book to know how to best approach conversations in a way that overcomes ingrained thought patterns and other barriers to seeking help when needed. This book is understandable, eloquent, and on point, making accessible to everyone cognitive-behavioral and motivational skills that until now have largely been the purview of health professionals. It fills a critical gap in the literature, highlighting the important role that everyone can play in helping to reduce stigma and barriers to mental health care.

My career in psychiatry has largely been working with military and veteran populations where the stigma of receiving mental health care has long been ingrained in thought processes such as, "I'll be seen as weak"; "My leaders or peers will treat me differently"; "I'll lose my security clearance"; "It will harm my career"; or "I should be able to handle problems on my own." When my research team provided the first detailed numbers in 2004 on the psychological impact of the wars in Iraq and Afghanistan, national news stories fixated on the prevalence rates we reported of PTSD and depression.

However, the most important part of that story, much less emphasized in the news, was that only 20 percent of service members with these conditions were willing to receive help. Since then, the field has come a long way toward improving stigma perceptions and facilitating access to care through screening and education campaigns, though we still have a ways to go; barriers remain, as they do in civilian society. What has been missing all along is a straightforward step-by-step guide, such as this one, for family members, friends, co-workers and even many health professionals, on how to most effectively have conversations around the topic of help seeking. This is a book I wish we had available when we first started studying stigma twenty years ago early in the Iraq and Afghanistan war era.

*Choosing Help* draws from Dr. Stecker's years of experience working in the field of suicide prevention, and provides detailed examples, including poignant relatable dialogues that bring to life the inner thought processes of resistance, and the specific words and phrases we can use to help someone begin to see other options they may not have considered or dismissed outright. This book provides clear guidance on effective communication strategies that can open the door to change, or at least improve the chances someone will be willing to consider initial steps in receiving the help they need. This could also be a roadmap for healthy communication in general. The world certainly can benefit now from more empathetic, respectful, genuine listening approaches. When you try out these skills with those in your life you're concerned about, you might find these tools seeping into other interactions. It's a whole new approach to conversation that truly meets people where they are.

—Charles W. Hoge, M.D., Colonel (Ret), U.S. Army & author of *Once a Warrior Always a Warrior: Navigating the Transition from Combat to Home*

# CHAPTER 1

# TALKING TO SOMEONE ABOUT GETTING HELP

SOME PEOPLE BELIEVE that, once the pain gets bad enough, that's when one will ask for help. While severity of the pain one feels *is* somewhat related to treatment seeking, it is often insufficient to motivate one to come in. We all know someone who never got help and suffered. They can have health, work, relationship, legal, financial, housing, eating, sleeping, and even breathing difficulties and still will not seek help.

Despite this, the medical community is structured so that people need to advocate for their own treatment. In fact, if you try to get help for your loved one with a mental health or substance abuse related disorder, you will commonly be turned away. The individual needs to ask for help themselves, even if they've lost the insight to do this on their own. **This book provides a roadmap for people who need help but who delay or resist treatment.**

Over 20+ years of intervening people who need mental health or substance use treatment but who refused to get help, I have learned the following:

- People often don't seek help because they believe getting help will be *uncomfortable*.

- People may prefer to suffer (even if it is extreme) as long as they don't have to ask for help.

- People have the capacity to change their mind about getting help.

- Changing thoughts about getting help can change everything and improve lives.

*Choosing Help* is meant to serve as a roadmap to understand why people don't get help for mental health and substance use concerns and how to encourage them to change their mind. The approach this book takes is straightforward and has been studied extensively in multiple clinical trials. The approach promotes a strategy to effectively listen to someone and help them change their mind on seeking help.

The method of helping someone change their mind on getting help (CBT-TS or CBT for Treatment Seeking) has been tested in more than ten clinical research trials (funded from the National Institutes of Health, the Department of Veterans Affairs, and the Department of Defense) in people with various conditions including: posttraumatic stress disorder (PTSD), substance use disorders, depression and suicidality. Regardless of condition, a common set of beliefs emerges on why people often don't seek help.

These beliefs include:

1.  They believe treatment won't work.

2.  They refuse a certain type of treatment.

3.  They say it will be hard or uncomfortable and want to avoid feeling that way.

4.  They want to handle problems on their own.

5.  They say they are not ready.

6.  They are concerned over perceived stigma.

7.  They say they don't "need" help.

8.  They say they don't have the time or money for treatment.

*Choosing Help* provides the building blocks for effective communication, how to talk with someone about getting help, and how to have specific conversations depending on why someone is not getting help. I will outline 20+ different ways to approach a discussion on help-seeking (see Chapter 2 for the full list). These include discussions about when help is needed, what kind of help is needed or wanted, coping strategies, listing pros/cons of seeking help, etc. Talking about thoughts on these aspects can help people make better decisions on whether or not they will get help. Each chapter outlines 1) strategies for talking through a particular barrier to help-seeking (i.e., stigma) and 2) first-person stories to demonstrate how to use the strategies. The stories show how anyone (family members, friends, doctors, neighbors, or even a stranger) can talk to someone about seeking help.

# A BIT OF BACKGROUND

This book is necessary because mental health and substance use concerns are ubiquitous, touching nearly all of us in one way or another, either personally or our family members or close friends. The vast majority of individuals who need help do not seek help, and in general, people will not get better if they do not seek help for these concerns.

## MENTAL HEALTH AND SUBSTANCE USE DISORDERS ARE COMMON

About 1 out of every 5 individuals (between 20–22 percent) experience a mental health or substance use disorder at some point in their lives. This includes disorders such as major depression, anxiety, PTSD, and drug/alcohol dependence. Approximately 5–7 percent experience a serious mental health condition, including disorders such as schizophrenia or bipolar disorder.

Evidence-based treatments, such as therapy and medications, exist for these conditions, improving symptoms, functioning, and quality of life. Which treatments work best for any specific person depends on many factors, including individual preference. Data suggest that individuals do best in treatment if they participate in decision-making about their treatment and are given the treatment they prefer.

For information on evidence-based treatments for mental health conditions, please visit websites such as NIAAA, NIDA, NIMH, AFSP, NAMI, WebMD, APA, or other sources that provide the most up to date information. Additional information on resources is available in this book in Chapter 11.

## PEOPLE DON'T GET HELP

The majority of people with mental health and substance use disorders do not seek treatment. As many as 75 percent of people who die by suicide never seek treatment, and between 50 and 75 percent of people with other mental health and substance use conditions never seek care. Even for those who do seek treatment, many delay getting help which may cause unnecessary suffering. In general, people fit into one of three groups with respect to treatment seeking: about a third go to treatment immediately; another third delay treatment, thinking that things might get better on their own; and about a third do not consider getting treatment at all—even if they are experiencing catastrophic symptoms. The approach outlined in this book is designed for individuals who delay or do not consider treatment for mental health and substance use concerns.

# SKILLS & ATTRIBUTES TO GUIDE CONVERSATIONS ON HELP-SEEKING

In order to talk with someone about getting help for a mental health or substance use problem, certain skills are helpful for healthy and effective communication, and helping individuals to feel heard and understood. You can't effectively communicate if you do not take the time to understand someone's point of view. Some people are easy to talk to; some are hard. And, because we bring our biases to every interaction, these skills allow for easier communication with anyone.

These four skills are:

1.  Empathy
2.  Genuineness
3.  Positive Regard
4.  Active Listening

**Empathy** is the capacity to understand someone else's point of view. You do not need to agree with their point of view, but having empathy is defined as being able to see the world from someone else's perspective. It is the act of validating or acknowledging their perspective.

Examples of empathy include tearing up when you see someone else's suffering; feeling joy when you see someone happy; feeling pain watching someone suffer.

In terms of help-seeking, being empathic means that you are able to put yourself in someone else's shoes enough to understand their situation from their point of view (not yours). You might meet someone who has a different lifestyle than you do. This might be someone who has a serious addiction to drugs or alcohol or a gambling problem or someone who is morbidly obese and has an addiction to food. When one is different than you, are *you* capable of putting yourself in their shoes to see their point of view? Do you judge them without considering the circumstances that led them to make their choices? Are you able to have a conversation with them to find out more about their thoughts and behaviors that contributed to their current situation? Do you make assumptions without checking in with them to see if the assumptions are accurate? Empathy is the capacity to see and feel the other person's point of view and is essential for productive discussion.

**Genuineness** is also essential for good communication. To communicate well, you need to be your authentic self. For example, you can tell when you hug someone how they feel about the hug. You can tell if they love a good, long, strong connecting hug or if they want it to end quickly. Being genuine is being your true self (which may mean saying no to a hug).

We sense when someone is not being genuine. We all know people who are over the top during basic conversation. They might be overly effusive when just saying hello or respond to a greeting on the weather with extreme emotion not appropriate to the situation. It's easier to accept someone who is overly effusive when we know that they truly have joyful energy, but when they force it, it can be off putting. Conversely, we know people who have difficulty being kind even if they adore someone. They might grunt as a hello because they have difficulty expressing their true feelings. Consider your own capacity to be genuine and when and in what situations you struggle with authenticity? Being genuine is the ability to be one's true self in every situation.

**Positive regard** is the capacity to show respect to another person. Respect is the ability to give others the same consideration you would give yourself. It's the ability to accept others and hold value for them even if you don't agree with them. Think about hair, for example. There are multiple ways a person can wear their hair. Hair can change colors, lengths, and styles. Choices about hair do not change the individual, even if the choices make the person look different. Can you value someone regardless of their hair? When do you lose respect for that person? Are you able to value someone with different political beliefs or parenting styles as you? Do you respect someone even if they cheer for an opposing football team or have a different faith? What if someone has a violent, criminal history? Perhaps there are factors that contributed to choices made. It's important to understand these factors with respect. Judgement is not necessary, nor helpful. Holding value for someone does not mean that you agree with their choices.

Positive regard and respect are critically important for healthy communication. Judgment rarely gets the job done and can even push people away. Positive regard can be demonstrated by giving others the opportunity to make their own choices. It can be shown verbally and non-verbally. Examples include making good eye contact, not walking away when someone is talking, not rolling your eyes, not interrupting people when they are talking, not criticizing, having a calm presence etc. **Positive regard is also critically important towards oneself**. We can NOT communicate effectively inside our own head about ourselves if we don't give ourselves respect. We are all doing the best we can at any given time with the knowledge that we currently have. We also all have the ability to evolve and do better.

**Active listening** is arguably the most important aspect of effective communication, is often overlooked, and vastly underutilized.

Active listening requires three steps:

1. Hear the words the other person is saying.

2. Process the words the other person is saying.

3. Communicate back to the person your understanding of what you heard them say.

This means that you have to use your ears, brain, and mouth (AND IN THAT ORDER!). Your ears need a moment to hear the words. Your brain needs a moment to process what your ears just heard, and your mouth needs a moment to communicate back, nonjudgmentally, an understanding of what you just heard. For example, if someone says, "I am mad," you activate all three steps to engage in active listening. First, your ears hear the three words, "I am mad." Second, your brain understands that they are telling you that they are feeling anger at that moment. Third, your mouth says something back like, "I hear you saying that you're mad right now. Do you want to talk more about that?" or "Sounds like you are feeling mad right now. What's going on for you?"

The reason why it's important to communicate an understanding of what you just heard is because we are incredibly *inaccurate* when it comes to our listening skills. Often, instead of hearing what the person is saying, we make assumptions about what we hear. We might think something like, "Ugh, they are mad at me again," even if they are not mad at you. Or we might think, "I've heard about their anger and I don't want to hear it again," even if that's not what they are referring to. Or worse, we might think something like, "I don't care what they are mad at," even in circumstances when their statement was in response to a question you may have asked them, like, "How are you?"

Active listening can't occur if you are more interested in talking. Consider this, if you are the type of person who likes to talk, you want someone to hear you. Otherwise, you're just talking to throw words out into the air that have no audience. Be the audience for another person just like you expect if you are the one doing the talking. Effective communication happens when both individuals can actively listen and communicate with each other. Remember ears, brain, mouth, in that order.

Overall, being **empathic, genuine**, and **respectful** help guide productive conversations where two individuals can **actively listen** to each other. These four components are necessary for healthy communication.

# THE RELATIONSHIP BETWEEN THINKING AND DOING

## HOW TO GET SOMEONE TO CHANGE THEIR MIND (EVEN IF THEY DON'T WANT TO)

**Cognitive-behavioral techniques (CBT)** are used in therapy to help individuals understand 1) why they engage in certain behaviors and 2) how to change their behaviors. The main idea behind the theory is that thoughts, behaviors, and feelings are all interconnected. Therefore, if we know what someone thinks about something, we know what they are likely to do. Importantly, the theory demonstrates that if we can understand how someone thinks, we might be able to change how they think, and that will change their behavior. Thus, if we understand someone's thoughts about help-seeking, we can help their decision about seeking help.

CBT has been used to treat a variety of conditions including depression, anxiety, posttraumatic stress disorder, insomnia, pain, and eating disorders. Here's a visual representation of how the process works:

What we think affects
how we act and feel

Thought

CBT

Emotion ———————— Behaviour

What we feel affects
how we think and do

What we do affects how
we think and feel

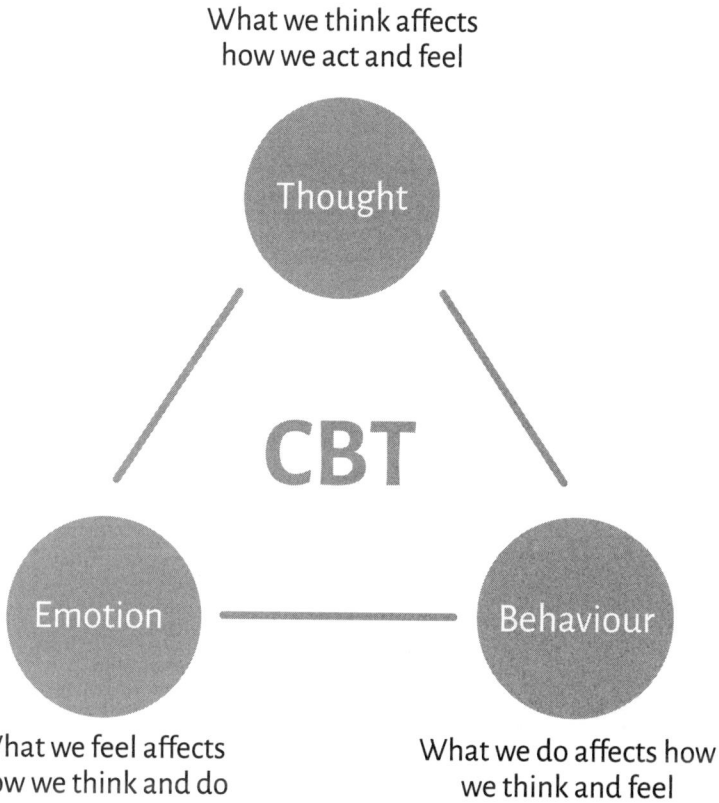

*The Cognitive-Behavioral Model (CBT) for understanding the relationship between thoughts, feelings and behaviors.*

Let me provide a couple of examples of how thoughts, behaviors, and feelings are interconnected.

**EXAMPLE 1:** Let's say you are driving down the highway and your favorite song comes on. You might turn up the volume, sing loudly, and even increase your speed. Suddenly blue lights come on behind you. How do your thoughts, feelings, and behaviors change?

| INITIAL THOUGHTS |
| --- |
| "I love this song!" |
| "I sing better when the music is loud!" |

| INITIAL FEELINGS |
| --- |
| Joyful |
| Playful |

| INITIAL BEHAVIORS |
| --- |
| Crank up the music |
| Sing loudly |
| Speed up |

Blue lights coming on behind you, however, may present an opportunity to change your thoughts. Instead of feeling the joy, you might think:

| NEW THOUGHTS |
| --- |
| "What the heck?" |
| "I'd better slow down." |
| "Why are they after me? They should be going after real criminals!" |

| NEW FEELINGS |
| --- |
| Anxious |
| Mad |

| NEW BEHAVIORS |
| --- |
| Turn down the music |
| Stop singing |
| Put hands back on the wheel |
| Slow down |

If the blue lights then go around you and speed down the high-way, your thoughts might again change. They might change to something like, "That's right! Go get the real criminal!" This new thought might also change your feelings and behaviors. You might feel relief. You might crank that song right back up and sing again. Maybe not so loudly, or maybe even louder!

The thoughts and behaviors are connected. When the thought was, "I love this song," the person drove without regard to speed or loudness. When the thought was, "Why is this cop behind me?" the person drove slower and stopped singing. Thoughts and behaviors were connected.

**EXAMPLE 2:** At age 8, my son played his first year of tackle football. I was a little nervous, so I attended his practices. At one practice it started raining. I thought, "They are going to pack up and send these kids home now. It's raining." They didn't. It started raining hard, but practice went on. It was raining so hard it was difficult to see which kid was mine. The rain blurred everything through my windshield. I thought, "What is happening?" "This kid is going to be a muddy mess," and "My son is not going to like this." I even considered getting out of my car (with my umbrella) to get him. When practice ended (45 minutes later!), my son walked over, got into my car, and exclaimed, "This is the best day of my life!" My thoughts, feelings and behaviors while in the car watching a rainy practice went like this:

| INITIAL THOUGHTS |
|---|
| "They will cancel practice because it is raining." |
| "Rain is a muddy mess." |
| "My son is not going to like this." |
| **INITIAL FEELINGS** |
| Worried |
| Anxious |
| **INITIAL BEHAVIORS** |
| Watched the practice like a hawk for 45 minutes trying to make sure that I could see what was happening. |

New information became available when my son exclaimed the rainy practice as the "best day of his life." This new information changed my thoughts. My new thought then changed the way that I felt and behaved for future practices.

| NEW THOUGHTS |
|---|
| "Practicing in the rain is fun." |
| "While rain may be a muddy mess to me, some people like muddy messes." |
| "He's going to be okay." |
| **NEW FEELINGS** |
| Joyful |
| A little embarrassed |
| **NEW BEHAVIORS** |
| Let go of the worry and started to enjoy his tackle football experience. |

As a sidenote, during the drive to his next practice, he closed his eyes and put both of his hands together by his face. I asked him what he was doing, and he said, "Praying for rain."

The point of these examples is to demonstrate how thoughts, feelings and behaviors are interconnected. When we change one, we have the opportunity to change the other two. Therefore, **the power to change a thought is the power to change any behavior**.

Moreover, the power to change a thought is the power to change any behavior, *even if you don't want to change*. We have all had a strongly held belief about something and changed our minds. Maybe you learned new information or maybe over time you learned other things that replaced or dulled or brightened the shine of the original thing. Thoughts can change. Despite this, we believe our thoughts (and believe them strongly), but the truth is that thoughts are just thoughts. We recognize new or additional information and can change our thoughts.

Once we change our thought, it can be hard to go back to the old thought. For example, think about something that you used to love to eat. Remember a food that was special or had some sort of magical power for you (in your head anyway). At some point, perhaps, the thought about that food changed. Changing that thought resulted in different feelings and behaviors for that food. One summer, I loved zucchini. Until a day when the zucchini tasted bitter. The bitter bite changed everything. I don't eat it anymore. My thought changed from, "Zucchini tastes good!" to, "Zucchini tastes bad." That one thought changed my feelings and behaviors regarding zucchini.

I know someone who smoked cigarettes throughout her early adulthood. She worked at a hospital and was aware of the hazards associated with smoking. It wasn't until someone told her that cigarettes would stain her teeth yellow that she considered changing her behavior. The thought that smoking could stain her teeth changed her feelings and behaviors with respect to smoking and the result was that she quit the habit.

The same instantaneous change in thoughts/feelings/behaviors can occur for anything, including a change in perspective about seeking help. Consider the individual who has been using substances for years. This individual might believe that without their substance of choice, they will die. They spend every day seeking or thinking or recovering from the use of their substance of choice. This individual is unlikely to want to go to treatment because they fully believe that they will DIE without their substance. A change in belief from, "I will die with my substance" to, "If I get help, I could survive without my substance" changes everything. This book will illustrate thoughts about seeking help and how we can purposefully change these thoughts in order to change help-seeking behavior.

# KEY SUMMARY POINTS

The main idea of this chapter is to provide information on key skills and attributes needed to have productive discussion regarding help-seeking for mental health and substance use disorders. Changing a thought about seeking help can save a life.

- Empathy is the ability to see the world from someone else's perspective.

- Genuineness is being free to be your true authentic self.

- Positive regard is being respectful to yourself and others.

- Active listening is a three-step process necessary for truly listening to another person.

- CBT is a process of understanding the relationship between how you think about seeking help and how you actually seek help.

# CHAPTER 2

# STARTING THE DISCUSSION: A THREE-STEP PROCESS

THIS CHAPTER OUTLINES ways to start and have a conversation with someone about the decision of whether or not to get help in a three-step process.

**The Three-Step Process**

1. Ask what their thoughts are on getting help
2. Listen to what they say about their thoughts on getting help
3. Talk about their thoughts on getting help

## STEP 1: ASK ABOUT THEIR THOUGHTS ON GETTING HELP

If you or someone you love is struggling with a mental health or substance use concern and you want to talk to them about getting help, **ask them their thoughts on getting help**.

| DON'T SAY | SAY |
|---|---|
| "You should get help." | "Have you been thinking about getting help?" |
| "Go see a doctor." | "What are your thoughts on getting help?" |
| "If I were you, I'd get help." | What are your thoughts about treatment? |

# STEP 2: LISTEN TO THEIR RESPONSE

As indicated in Chapter 1, there are a variety of reasons why individuals indicate that seeking help is not for them. By **listening to their responses** to questions regarding their current feelings towards treatment, you can better address their concerns.

They include:

1. They don't believe treatment will work.
2. They refuse a certain type of treatment.
3. They say it will be hard or uncomfortable and want to avoid the feeling.
4. They want to handle it on their own.
5. They say they are not ready.
6. They are concerned over perceived stigma.
7. They say they don't "need" help.
8. They say they don't have the time or money for treatment.

This list contains the most common reasons why someone doesn't go to treatment. They might say something outside of this list or they might say multiple reasons from this list. It's important to hear their thoughts.

## STEP 3: TALK ABOUT THEIR THOUGHTS ON SEEKING HELP

With your newfound insight into their underlying concerns about seeking treatment, it's now time to sit down and **have an informed conversation** about getting the help they need. Each of the subsequent chapters identifies one of the main reasons why someone hesitates to go to treatment and breaks down how to have a discussion about this thought. Each chapter outlines specific strategies for discussions to be productive. For example, just because someone says they don't have time to get help, doesn't necessarily mean they don't have time to get help. Under normal circumstances, you might not challenge someone's thoughts about time. And ultimately, it will always be an individual choice of whether or not to get help. The outlined strategies for productive discussions should not be hostile or confrontational, but instead used as guides to understand why someone might resist help despite their struggle. Talking it through might help them change their mind.

## WHY TALKING ABOUT TREATMENT IS IMPORTANT

Often, there is a noticeable difference between the initial reaction to the thought of getting help and simply thinking through whether or not getting help is an *option*. It's important to discuss thoughts about getting help in more detail because the initial thought isn't necessarily "true."

Sometimes it's just an instant reaction to something new. Often, and especially if we are feeling uncomfortable, we say no. The no isn't really a no, it's an automatic reaction. Talking it through allows for a more thorough assessment of if, where, when, what, and why someone might get help.

The following list contains **the most common reasons why someone isn't getting help and suggestions for how to talk to them about the reason**. Each Chapter (3–10) focuses on each of these eight reasons for not going to treatment. Each chapter also shares a story to illustrate how to talk about getting help related to that reason. Any of the suggested talking points about getting help (outlined in the table below) could be important for any individual, however; the suggested talking points may correspond best with that particular reason, based on our experience. For example, if someone indicated that they were not interested in getting help because of "stigma," you could have a discussion with them about confidentiality and overcoming obstacles.

## COMMON THOUGHTS ABOUT GETTING HELP AND HOW TO TALK ABOUT THEM

| REASON FOR NOT GETTING HELP | HOW TO TALK ABOUT EACH THOUGHT OR CONCERN |
|---|---|
| I only want a certain type of treatment. | Acknowledge what they don't want |
|  | Identify what they do want |
| I don't need help. | Define what treatment is |
|  | Identify what it means to "need" help |
|  | Identify WHEN help is needed |
|  | Pros of getting help; cons of getting help |
| I can handle it on my own. | Identify their plan for treatment |
|  | You are on your own |
|  | Identify coping skills |
|  | Utilize support system |
| Treatment is too hard, intense. | Identify and feel the feelings |
|  | Identify facts/acceptance |
| There's too much stigma. | Confidentiality |
|  | Overcoming obstacles |
|  | Underdogs are heroes |
| Treatment won't work. | Define treatment |
|  | Identify treatment options |
|  | Research treatment effectiveness |
|  | Identify treatment goals |
| No time or money for treatment. | Identify facts |
|  | Cost/benefit analysis |
| Not ready for treatment/not ready to quit drinking. | Coping strategies |
|  | Readiness |
|  | Communication skills |
|  | Cost/benefit analysis |

# HOW TO CHANGE A THOUGHT

The best predictor of whether someone will get help is whether they think treatment will benefit them; thus it's important to understand thoughts about getting help. Knowing someone's thoughts about getting help presents opportunities to think through the choice more fully. Given that their thoughts about getting help might be automatic, they are worth discussing and potentially changing.

**To change a thought, you have to understand the extent to which they believe their thought is true.**

We all have thoughts we believe are categorically and undeniably true. Some of these thoughts are "true," while some have room for change. Thoughts can change with more information, or over time, or when seen in a different context. For example, it would be easy for a parent to identify with the thought, "I love my child." It might be hard to imagine having any other thoughts about your child except, "I love this child." On any given day, if you ask them if they love their child, they will say, "Yes! 100 percent." There might be a moment; however, when other thoughts emerge besides, "I love this child." The thought might change from, "I love this child" to, "I love this child, but parenting is hard." It doesn't mean the thought, "I love this child" is no longer true, it means that thoughts are fluid and have the capacity to change over time and in different contexts. During some particularly trying teenage or toddler years, the thought might even momentarily become, "I don't like this child."

Thoughts are just thoughts. They can change. Any thought about anything has the capacity for change. Consider this in the context of help-seeking. Someone might think that they can't seek treatment for a substance use concern because they believe they need to be fully ready to stop before they get help. If the thought changes from, "I need to be 100 percent ready to stop before getting help" to, "I would like to work with someone to get ready to quit," they might be more likely to seek professional help.

To better understand the extent to which someone believes their thought is true, ask the following questions:

- Where did they learn that thought?
- Is there evidence for/against that thought?
- How true is the thought?
- Do they apply this same thought to other people that they know? If not, under what circumstances does the thought change?
- What is the cost of having that thought? What is the benefit of having that thought?

Here are some examples demonstrating these questions with respect to thoughts about seeking help.

## CASE #1

**What are your thoughts on seeking help?**
I don't need help.

**What does needing help mean to you?**
It's weak.

**Where did you learn it was weak to need help?**
I'm not sure. I learned as a kid not to ask for help.

**Is there any instance where getting help is smart?**
I'd ask for help if I were having a heart attack.

This example demonstrates an opportunity to explore someone's thoughts on getting help. This discussion could open the door or lead to a more in-depth discussion on seeking help.

## CASE #2

**What are your thoughts on seeking help?**
I don't want to go to a doctor because they will prescribe a medicine and I don't want to be on a medicine.

**If you sought help, is medicine the only option for treatment?**
I don't think so. I think I could do therapy.

**You don't have to take medicine. Would you prefer to go to therapy?**
I think it would be good to talk to someone about what's been going on for me.

In Case #2, the individual may not have considered treatment at all because they thought it meant that a doctor would try to prescribe them medication. In reality, they were open to the idea of therapy but didn't realize it was an option. Just having this discussion could open a door to considering options for help.

Both examples demonstrate how to talk with someone about their thoughts on getting help. You can explore what the thought means to them, where they learned that thought, how true the thought is, etc.

# CHANGING THE THOUGHT

If the thought isn't helpful, what would be helpful for that person?

If you are talking with someone and they state, "I don't need help because my situation isn't bad enough to seek treatment. At least I still function at my job," you can check the "truth" of this thought. Let's say you ask them how true the above sentence is, and they say it is 100 percent true. It might be true that they are still functioning at their job. What might also be true is that their family relationships and other important social relationships are not doing as well. Perhaps their health or their optimism for life is poor. Take in the whole picture of the individual and help them see the bigger context. If they are indeed functioning well socially, and at work, and with their health, then perhaps they don't need help. If they are having significant impairment in one or more of these areas, then it might do them well to consider the overall big picture.

Changing someone's way of thinking requires:

- A discussion about their perspective.
- Open communication between the two (or more) parties.
- Empathic, authentic, respectful, active listening (see Chapter 1).
- Acceptance of their strategy to manage their life.

Remember these questions to engage in a conversation about how they view seeking help:

- Where did they learn that thought?

- Is there evidence for/against that thought?

- How true is the thought?

- Do they apply this same thought to other people that they know? If not, under what circumstances does the thought change?

- What is the cost of having that thought? What is the benefit of having that thought?

Now, here are some examples of conversations to change someone's perspective on seeking help.

## EXAMPLE 1: CHANGING THOUGHTS ABOUT AN INDIVIDUAL'S STRENGTHS

People who struggle with depression and low self-esteem often have difficulty identifying their strengths. If you ask someone with depression, "What are your strengths? What are you good at?" you will likely hear the response, "Nothing. I'm not good at anything." Further discussion regarding this could be helpful. How true is it that they are good at nothing? Is it true that they have never been good at anything in their whole life? The discussion probably will reveal that they possess some strengths. Maybe they can make scrambled eggs or play the piano or enjoy singing. This is a starting point to generate a reality-based list of their strengths.

They may say things like:

- I'm good with animals

- I like my hands

- I'm good at washing a car

- I can sing

- I'm a good driver

- The color purple looks okay on me

- I'm a good writer

- I know how to read people

Once a realistic list of strengths is identified, it's no longer possible that "I'm not good at anything" is 100 percent true. The thought could change to "I'm good at a couple of things" or "I wish I was better at certain things, but I'm good at some things" or, "I'm good at a couple of things, but struggle with self-esteem. I'd like to work on it."

**Original Thought: I'm not good at anything**

**New Thought: I'm good at a couple of things**

This might sound like a minor tweak in a sentence, but minor tweaks have the power to change behavior and the power to change the course of someone's entire life. It can change brain chemistry and a person's outlook and a person's motivation to try.

## EXAMPLE 2: APPLYING THIS STRATEGY TO CHANGE SOMEONE'S THOUGHT ABOUT SEEKING HELP

Another example of how to change someone's thought happens when working with an individual in treatment for an alcohol use disorder. They might say something like: "Only someone who has been there can help me." Below is one example of how to potentially modify this thought:

**Andy:** Only someone who has been there can help me.

**Bob:** How true is it that only someone who has been there can help you?

**Andy:** 100 percent true.

**Bob:** Is there any evidence that this is true?

**Andy:** Yes, AA is based on this premise and in treatment they put you in groups with others struggling with addiction.

**Bob:** Is there any evidence against this thought being true?

**Andy:** None that I can think of.

**Bob:** Would you tell someone else you cared about who was addicted to alcohol that they should only work with people with alcohol use disorders?

**Andy:** Well, I'm not sure. People with alcohol problems don't always work the program and might not *all* be helpful. I'd tell them to work with anyone who is honestly working their program.

**Bob:** Okay, how does a sober person who never had an alcohol problem fit into the equation? Someone who is not actively drinking to cope with life stress or drinking to numb emotions or to head off withdrawal? Would they be an appropriate support person in any capacity?

**Andy:** They don't understand what it is like to "be" there. They don't know the struggle.

**Bob:** Is it their job to "be" there (struggle with alcohol) or is it their job to help with tools to NOT "be" there? Could they be helpful with that part?

**Andy:** Okay, maybe if they truly get it and are not judgmental.

**Bob:** Okay, so the thought, "Only someone who has been there can help me" is not 100 percent true, but is mostly true from your perspective?

**Andy:** Maybe it's more like, "I prefer working with individuals who truly understand alcohol use disorders."

> **Original Thought: Only someone**
> **who has been there can help.**
>
> **New Thought: I prefer working with people**
> **who truly understand alcohol use disorders.**

## SUMMARY OF THE THREE-STEP PROCESS FOR DISCUSSIONS ABOUT SEEKING HELP:

1.  Ask their thoughts on getting help

2.  Listen to their thoughts on getting help

3.  Talk about their thoughts on getting help (changing thoughts when applicable).

| THREE-STEP PROCESS FOR GUIDING DISCUSSIONS ||
|---|---|
| 1. What are your thoughts on getting help? | I don't have time. |
|  | I can handle it on my own. |
| 2. Acknowledge thoughts | They feel they don't have time for treatment. They prefer to handle it on their own. |
| 3. Further discussions about thoughts | Where did they learn that thought? |
|  | Is there evidence for/against that thought? |
|  | How true is the thought? |
|  | Do they apply this same thought to other people that they know? If not, under what circumstances does the thought change? |
|  | What is the cost of having that thought? What is the benefit of having that thought? |

# COGNITIVE DISTORTIONS

In any discussion focused on understanding how someone thinks, it's important to recognize cognitive distortions. These are thinking patterns that emerge when people are stressed and can become automatic ways of thinking over time. Cognitive distortions are patterns of thinking that are not entirely based in reality or facts, but instead are automatic ways of responding to situations.

For example, for those who read any of the Winnie the Pooh series, each of the characters has an "automatic" way of viewing the world. Eeyore tends to see the sadness or defeat in the situation. Piglet responds with anxiety. Owl tries to apply logic and avoid feelings. Tigger is defensive and justifies play. These patterns of thinking can explain why someone tends to think the worst during times of stress (catastrophizing) while others refuse to see the situation even when it is right in front of them (denial). Our automatic thoughts about help-seeking can follow these same thinking styles or cognitive distortions. We all have them. **They become problematic when an individual is unaware that they are applying them and not considering other ways of seeing the situation.**

Below is a list of common distortions and how they may be applied to help-seeking.

- **Catastrophizing:** Assuming the worst.
  - ○ "If I talk about what happened to me in treatment, I'll go insane."
  - ○ "If I go to treatment, I'll lose my job and family."
- **Denial:** Believing something is true despite overwhelming evidence to the contrary.
  - ○ "I am not addicted."
  - ○ "I don't have a problem."

- **Minimizing:** Positive or negative aspects of the situation are minimized.

  o "Even though I need to take illegal drugs multiple times a day every day just to not go through withdrawal, at least I'm still taking time to be with my children, so I don't need help."

- **All-or-nothing thinking:** Seeing one extreme or the other in a situation. Black or white without seeing the shades of grey. Typically, people who have all or nothing thinking have unrealistic standards and may miss the complexity of most situations.

  o "If I go to treatment, it means that I am crazy."

- **Overgeneralization:** Taking one instance and applying it to all future instances. All instances will have the same outcome.

  o "My uncle went to treatment and was hospitalized so I can't go to treatment because they will hospitalize me."

- **Mental filter:** Focusing on negative aspects only.

  o "If I go to treatment, it will be uncomfortable."

- **Should/must:** Unreasonable demands placed on self for a situation.

  o "I should handle it on my own."

- **Emotional reasoning:** Drawing conclusions based on feelings rather than facts.

  o "I feel like it won't work out if I go to treatment because it will be hard."

- **Labeling:** Putting a label on something or someone.
  - ○ "Only crazy people seek help."
  - ○ "Only losers seek help."
- **Mind-reading:** Believing you know what someone else is thinking or feeling without having the data from them.
  - ○ "If I go to therapy, they are going to tell me to (insert whatever) and I don't need to hear that."
- **Forecasting/Jumping to conclusions/Predictive thinking:** Believing they know the outcome beforehand.
  - ○ "There is no point in going to treatment because I know what they are going to say, and it won't work."

Understanding cognitive distortions may help further guide discussions on help-seeking.

## ENABLING VS. HELPING

When someone we care about is in need, it's easy to want to help. Unfortunately, help can be helpful or it can be harmful. A full discussion about enabling is beyond the scope of this book, however; in general, enabling is engaging in behaviors that perpetuate (or even increase) problem behaviors in others. For example, giving a child a cookie every time they tantrum is going to increase the likelihood of tantrums. The goal might be to stop the tantrum in the immediate, but it ends up increasing the chances of future tantrums. Instead, an option might be to acknowledge the emotion of the situation and talk with the child about ways to communicate.

In the case of help-seeking, someone who enables others unintentionally prevents someone from getting treatment. Their intention might be to be helpful, however, the result is that their assistance ironically maintains the status quo. We can illustrate this with someone who gambles. Let's say the person who gambles loses their entire paycheck for the month from gambling. Therefore, they are not able to pay their bills that month. A concerned loved one might talk with them and help them to figure out options moving forward. The concerned loved one does not take direct action on the situation (or if they do, they do it only on a one-time basis). The person who enables, on the other hand, might pay the bills for the person who gambles or give them a place to live.

Typically, the person who enables becomes a part of the problem behavior or pattern long term. The person who enables may be trying to protect their loved one from consequences. Yet, facing consequences could help the person who gambles face the reality of their situation rather than sidestep it. This demonstrates how enabling can impede help-seeking.

## PUTTING IT ALL TOGETHER

Aaron is a 30-year-old veteran who served in the United States Army. He was deployed to Afghanistan and witnessed his friend die in combat. Upon returning to the States, Aaron struggled with sleeplessness, agitation, nightmares, increased drinking, and difficulty concentrating. He had difficulty participating in his work and family obligations due to a strong need to be with the family members of his friend who died. His family was increasingly concerned about Aaron's symptoms of PTSD and asked Aaron to consider getting help. Aaron refused to get help because of stigma and his concern that going to treatment would mean he would forget his friend. After discussing his thoughts in more detail, Aaron decided that he wanted to honor the memory of his friend, ensuring that he would never be forgotten and to go to treatment for his sleeplessness and nightmares. Instead of feeling stigma about seeking PTSD treatment, he decided to get help to honor his friend's memory.

Key things to consider when having a discussion with someone on getting help:

- Any of the strategies outlined can be used with any individual.
- Any of the strategies can be the starting point.
- The discussion topics can be in any order and individualized for that specific person.
- The goal of the discussion is to talk about getting help.
- Discussion helps to understand how a person thinks about treatment.
- There should be no judgement.
- Discussions can become highly emotional. If someone is defensive or emotions are too high, it's likely the discussion is no longer productive. Come back to it later.

An additional way to frame conversations focused on choosing help is by theme. For example, if someone does not believe they need help or isn't sure what treatment is, the table below may be a useful guide for conversation starters.

| HOW TO START A CONVERSATION ON GETTING HELP (BASED ON THEME) | |
| --- | --- |
| **CONVERSATION STARTERS** | **USE WHEN THEY BELIEVE...** |
| **NEEDING HELP** | |
| What does it mean to "need help?" | They don't need help |
| At what point will help be needed (WHEN?) | They don't need help |
| What are the facts/reality of the situation | No time/money |
| Can you accept facts/reality | Hard to open up |
| **DEFINING TREATMENT** | |
| Define what treatment is | Treatment won't work<br><br>They don't need help<br><br>Handling it on their own |
| Identify options for treatment | Treatment won't work |
| Research treatment effectiveness | Treatment won't work |
| Identify treatment goals | Treatment won't work |
| Identify what types of treatment are not a good fit for the individual | Only a certain type of treatment |
| Identify what types of treatment are a good fit for the individual | Only a certain type of treatment |

| HOW TO START A CONVERSATION ON GETTING HELP (BASED ON THEME) | |
| --- | --- |
| Write down specific treatment plan | Handling it on their own |
| Discuss treatment confidentiality | Stigma |
| Identify pros/cons of seeking treatment (risk/benefit analysis) | They don't need help |
| | No time/money |
| | Not ready for treatment |
| **COPING SKILLS/SUPPORT SYSTEM** | |
| Identify coping skills | Handling it on their own |
| | Not ready |
| Identify and use support system | Handling it on their own |
| Use of substances to cope | Not ready |
| **OTHER FACTORS TO CONSIDER AND DISCUSS** | |
| Overcoming obstacles is cool | Stigma |
| Underdogs are heroes | Stigma |
| Identify and feel the feelings | Hard to open up |
| | Not ready |
| You're on your own | Handling it on their own |
| Idea that you don't need to be better BEFORE getting help | Not ready |
| The use of alcohol to communicate | Not ready |

# KEY SUMMARY POINTS

The main idea of this chapter is identifying how to start a conversation with someone about the idea of getting help.

- Any of the conversation starters can be used. No single one/ strategy works best. It is best to fit the discussion to the specific individual.

- Some of the conversation starters fit well with certain belief systems.

- The whole point of the conversation is to talk about getting help.

- Engage in three-step process for discussion (ask thoughts about getting help, listen to thoughts, engage in discussion about thoughts for seeking help).

- No judgement.

- Whenever the emotion gets too hot in a discussion, take a break and come back to it later.

# CHAPTER 3

# "TREATMENT WON'T WORK"

**T**HIS CHAPTER HIGHLIGHTS how to talk to someone who isn't seeking help because they believe that treatment won't work for them. We begin with the story of Emily to illustrate an example of how to talk to someone who believes this thought. The chapter ends with suggestions for how to change someone's mind when they believe this thought.

## EMILY'S STORY: A CASE STUDY

I stare out the window for several minutes looking for the perfect moment. The blinds are slanted at just the right angle so light can still come in, but no one can see inside. I'm wearing a black hoody and a baseball cap and will keep my head down, walking fast, not running. Running would call attention. The right time of day is that gap when it's still a little light out but not dark. Dusk. And no one can be on the street. My street is somewhat busy even though I live in a small town.

I don't like to get my mail when anyone is walking or driving down my street. I know it's ridiculous. I know no one even cares, but I can't handle small talk. What's so easy for some people is really hard for me. No one is driving or walking by, so I take that moment to walk to the mailbox. In the mailbox is nothing except for one advertisement for a real estate agency. I should've known there wouldn't be anything important. I don't get much mail, but it would've driven me crazy to let it sit in the mailbox all night. On the walk back up the driveway, I hear a car coming. I hear myself squeal and throw myself into a bush. *Oh my lord Jesus*, I think, and feel sweat break out all over my body. It's too hot for a hoody, but I need it for cover. The bush is scratchy. I'm hot and now mortified. What if the driver saw me and saw me jump into a bush? And as I'm sitting there feeling foolish, my neighbor calls out, "Hi, dear."

How embarrassing. It's bad enough I can't even walk to the mailbox like a normal person, but now there is witness to this scene. I don't even have anyone or anything to hide from! It's just so uncomfortable talking to people. Or having people look at me. I don't like it when people look at me. And now my neighbor is looking at me.

"Hi, Bonnie." Bonnie is an 81-year-old woman who lives alone in the house next door. She is precious. Sweet and kind. She has a pleasant voice you'd expect from an angel who has seen it all and laughed through most of it with kindness and joy. Her husband died about 10 years ago. In her isolation, she sits on the front porch and watches the birds. Everyone in my town knows everyone else. She knows my parents and has known me since I was born. Actually, everyone knows my parents. They are successful and accomplished in their fields. Unlike me.

Considering I feel silly and have no idea how to pass this off as anything other than ridiculousness, I figure it best to stand up and walk back to my door. I hear her say, "Have a good evening" as I shut the door behind me. The door is already closed when I say back to her, "You, too."

Today has already not been a good day. I work at a bookstore. I love books, almost all genres. I began working at the bookstore while in college and stayed on after graduation. My parents expected that I would pursue more schooling, and actually, I would love to get my PhD in literature, but I'm not confident enough to send in my work for publication. Although encouraged by professors to continue writing, I'm a better reader than writer. And I couldn't handle sending in one of my manuscripts just to have it rejected. Maybe at some point I'll go back to school for my PhD, but not now.

Work was busy today. Saturdays are typically our busiest days because people are out of school and work and like to browse "downtown." In our small town there isn't much to do on weekends, so people socialize by walking around downtown, where the store is located. I don't mind busy days, and I like most of our customers. Today was different though. People were in a rush. And grumpy. We had a lot of crabby customers who expressed frustration over our small bookstore not having the precise book they wanted. Multiple times I heard them say they should have just ordered it online.

Well! How could they expect our one bookstore to have every book in the universe? It's absurd! Especially some of the more obscure books requested today! No sir, we do not have the book published in 1977 about the Appalachian Trail! I'm sorry ma'am but we do not currently have in stock a cookbook focused exclusively on sauerkraut! I feel terrible we could not make them happy because there is no greater feeling in the world than cracking open a new book. It's the greatest feeling in the world. That anticipation of entering a new adventure! I offered to look online and order the books for them, but the offers were poorly received. They indicated they were perfectly capable of searching online and ordering on their own.

Well then. Fine!

And while I was worrying about displeased customers, in walk two well-dressed, composed women. They were probably around age 30, so maybe 5 years older than I, but they seemed years ahead of me in terms of composure and confidence. In fact, they reminded me of my mother. No one makes me feel less confident than my mother. My mother's intelligence is off the charts. She is well known in her field of medical research. Having a scientist for a mother; however, is…difficult. I never quite measure up. She perceives emotions and feelings as irrational and in her mind, everything has a place and a purpose. When something lacks a place and purpose to *her*, like feeling sad because she threw away my favorite shoes because the soles were worn down, she waves it away as irrelevant.

I tried so hard to hold back my tears that day when I was 8 and my shoes were in the trash, but couldn't. She perceives me as emotional and dramatic. I never liked the new shoes she purchased to replace the old ones, even though they were similar in color and style. They never felt right. I was not allowed to cry (too dramatic) or make noise (she was working, and I should go play in my room) or eat certain foods (unless she portioned out the precise measurements of proteins, fats, and carbs). For me, there is nothing more satisfying than stuffing a piece of hot warm pizza down my throat, chewing, (barely and with reckless abandon), when my mother is not watching me. I suffer horrifying guilt and shame afterwards but can't resist the pleasure. I also carry an extra 15–20 pounds because of this reckless abandon with food, which displeases her immensely. I can't tell you how many times I've heard her say, "Emily, one must be prudent with one's body and take great care with nutrition." I know she's right, but I can't control myself like other people can.

After browsing, the women both purchased the new bestselling book we have featured in the front of the store. The author of this book is an internationally recognized local writer. When they were checking out, I said, "Excellent choice"!

"Have you read it?" one of them asked. She was wearing a tailored cashmere trench coat with a cream-colored cashmere sweater and long pants. She looked straight out of a catalog.

"I have. It was so good. It's one of those books that's hard to put down. I thought about it for days because it was so thought provoking," I replied.

"I'm looking forward to reading it. We chose it for our book club to read," the other stated.

I send them off with, "Enjoy!"

A short while later, there is a break in the busy-ness and I run next door to the coffee shop to grab a sandwich. The sandwiches at the coffee shop are not as good as the ones at the diner, but I can never show my face in the diner again. The last time, the busboy came to remove my empty plate and I said, "Love you" instead of, "Thank you" to him. His face turned as red as mine! I've never seen that busboy a day in my life and, if possible, I'd like to never see him again.

As I walk into the coffee shop, I notice the two women from the bookstore sitting at a table. They look up as I pass their table, smile, and say hello. I want to say hello back but outside the bookstore, I feel so awkward. Instead of, "Hi," out of my mouth comes a grumbled, horrible noise halfway between a "hello" and "good morning." It came out sounding something like, "Gollod."

Gollod?

The noise "gollod" sounds like I'm having a stroke. What if I am having a stroke? If I am having a stroke, would anyone know? Or help me? Would anyone here even know the symptoms of a stroke? Would they just look at me and try to move away as fast as possible in the event that whatever I have is contagious? Oh my gosh. If I am having a stroke, and I end up at the hospital, they could run tests and find that I have some other awful disease. Like cancer! That mole on my arm is actually melanoma and because I didn't get it checked, it metastasized, and cancer is all over my body. My God. I'm not having a stroke at all. I have cancer that has metastasized into my brain and I'm dying.

What if I only have a couple months left to live?

What if the last word I ever said to anyone was, 'Gollod?'

What would my mother think?

She'd be so mad that she wasn't the one to diagnose me. Actually, this IS her fault! If anyone should have been able to diagnose Stage 4 metastatic melanoma, it should have been *her*!

All this runs through my brain as I stand there with those two women gawking at me. Well! I'm not going to stand there and have them gawk at me during my final moments. I regain some semblance of self and turn to walk to the counter to order a coffee and a sandwich, but I'm too discombobulated and can't seem to remember how to walk. My walk feels weird. Is this another symptom of a stroke or cancer? I tell myself to put one foot in front of the other and end up doing some weird, stiff, march-like walk. By the time I get to the cashier, I'm so flustered that I just grab a couple of apples, pay for them, and leave. I very much wanted a sandwich instead.

These women have ruined my day.

I really do need to get that mole on my arm checked out by a doctor. What if I do have cancer?

Back at the bookstore, I snarf the apples and am surprised to find that my voice and walk have reappeared. I seem to be operating at a somewhat functional capacity, although I barely register the passing of time. Before I know it, I'm back in my living room waiting for the perfect moment to grab my mail.

The next day is Sunday, a day I typically visit my parents. They are having colleagues over for dinner tonight and have requested I come for lunch instead. My parents entertain often. My mother sits on committees and multiple influential advisory boards. She likes to be in charge. A leader in her field. My father, on the other hand, is not as interested in leadership as he is in investigating the science of how things work. At social gatherings, my mother politics and my father ponders.

When I arrive at my parents' home, my mother greets me with, "Emily, do take care when using the bathrooms. We have guests arriving." Do take care? What does she think, that I walk into a bathroom and only walk out once I have rendered it a disaster zone? Does she think I'm going to have explosive diarrhea, and it will be so explosive that it will leave dirty bits all over her sanitized bathroom? Actually, I do feel a bit gassy. Those apples yesterday didn't calm the bowels, and neither does my mother.

"I'll make sure to toot in there before I leave."

"Emily. Please don't be crass," she replies.

"One must be prudent with one's butthole," I utter under my breath. I can tell she hears as she stares me down, so I look away and try to focus on the meal presented, my heart pounding.

As their dinner tonight will be catered, and mother does not cook, we have salad and bread for lunch. I'm quite hungry and know that this meal will not satiate. As we sit to eat, I grab a roll and smear a slab of butter on my bread. "Do you really need that much butter on your bread, Emily?"

"Oh. I'm sorry. I guess I'm hungry."

"Please do control yourself, Emily," I hear her say as I begin to contemplate my stop through the McDonalds drive through on the way home. I probably shouldn't have McDonalds. Maybe I should just eat the salad? She does seem to understand nutrition and health whereas I am a mess. But I'm hungry. And I like butter. I like food. Who wouldn't like food? Food is delicious. And you have to eat. Why does she always need to control each and every little thing? How can she live trying to control everything all the time?

During lunch, my mother tells me about her advisory committee members and the new applications they will be reviewing. I can't focus on anything she is saying and try to get through the time with her as quickly as possible. At the end of the meal, my father walks me to my car and says, "You know she is just trying to help you."

"Yes, I know, Dad." I reach to kiss him on the cheek, and he asks me what book I am reading now. My father and I have always shared a love of books. He encouraged reading and would indulge me with weekly trips to the bookstore where I could pick out whichever books I wanted. To my mother's dismay, I often chose children and young adult books and would read them voraciously. She greatly preferred for me to read scientific books, but my father allowed age-appropriate adventures.

While his question as to which book I was reading was both routine and innocuous, I respond with, "WHAT DOES IT MATTER? Who cares if I'm reading romance novels or horror stories? What does it even matter?" I shout. I love my father dearly, but even so, I find myself jumping into the car, slamming the door, starting the car, and reeling out of their driveway like a bat out of hell.

I can't believe I just treated my father like that, but I needed to explode. I drive through both McDonalds *and* Dairy Queen on the way home.

Pulling into my driveway after the scene with my father, I see Bonnie sitting in the rocker on her porch next door. Still feeling bad about my ridiculousness yesterday, as I was hardly social, and my uncalled for rant today with my father, I walk over to chat with her for a moment. She lives alone and even though she has friends through church, she might feel lonely. It must be hard to lose a spouse. Charlie was a wonderful man too. He always smiled and said hello to everyone. So cheerful and kind.

"Hi, Miss Bonnie. How are you today?" I ask as I walk over to her.

"Well, hi there darling. I'm doing alright. How are you doing?" she replies.

"I'm good. Just got back from lunch with my parents."

"And how are they?" she asks me.

"Uh, well. Same as always. They have a function at their home tonight. Mom invited her board committee over."

"Ahh. She sure has been successful."

"Yes. Yes, she has. Well, it's been great to see you. Hope you have a wonderful rest of your day, Miss Bonnie!" I say as I turn to walk to my house.

"Emily?"

"Yes ma'am?"

"Excuse me for being presumptuous, but have you thought about getting help?"

"Help?"

"You seem a bit down. And a little jumpy," referring to my jumping into a bush like a freak yesterday.

"Oh. Oh that. That was just silly."

"Dear, I was a teacher for many years and have watched people struggle. And I've watched you through the years and know that you're a lovely young woman, and it seems you could use a bit of help."

"Well, if my mother couldn't fix me, nothing could."

"Have you thought about talking to someone?"

"Like a psychologist?"

"Do you think talking with a psychologist could help you?" she asks me.

"I don't think that would work for me. I mean, I'm sure seeing a therapist works for a lot of people, but I don't think it would work for me."

"Oh? What are your thoughts about psychologists?"

*'That they will think I'm insane. That they will think I need medication. That I won't be able to talk to them. Oh God, that I will be able to talk to them. I'll talk to them and say all sorts of ridiculous things. That they will stare at me. That they won't even be able to look at me because I'm so pathetic. That I will bore them.*

*That after all their training and expertise, there will be nothing they can do to fix me.'*

I think all this and then say, "Well, psychologists are fine and lots of people need them. I am not sure that there is anything they can say that would help me."

"What kinds of things do you think they would say?"

"Well. Gee. I don't actually know. Maybe that I worry too much?"

"You know as I get older, I worry less. Do you find yourself worrying a lot?"

"Sure. Just today I worried I might have cancer. Or had a stroke."

Smiling, she says, "I see. You don't seem like you had a stroke."

"Maybe. Maybe not."

"You know, I was your mother's teacher in 3rd grade. She was all wound up even back then. She worried all the time, about all sorts of things, and it made it hard for her to focus," she informs me.

I knew that Miss Bonnie was one of my mother's elementary school teachers, but I don't know much about my mother's childhood. She hardly talks about anything except her work and to chide me for my incompetence. "Yes, ma'am. My mom still seems to focus on every little thing. I don't want to end up like her, but I'm not sure how talking about it could help me. Maybe I can't be fixed."

"You're a lovely woman, Emily. There is nothing to fix. I just wondered if you thought about talking to someone about your anxiety. Maybe you could learn ways to become less worried."

"I don't see how talking to someone would help."

"If you were to talk with someone, what would you talk about? What would you want to work on?"

Several things go through my mind in an instant. I think about jumping in the bush yesterday because being seen walking up my own driveway felt like firecrackers had just gone off next to me. I think about the guttural nonsense that came out of my mouth today at the coffee shop and how my brain spun out and tried to kill me with metastatic melanoma. I think about the scene at my parents' house where I yelled at my dad for no reason. I consider the millions of times I was unable to speak or act because it all felt too much. I also think about how overwhelming it would be to even start. Just making the phone call to schedule an appointment would trigger a panic attack and potential 911 emergency. I admit, "It would be nice not to have panic attacks."

"Maybe you could find a psychologist who focuses on working with individuals with panic attacks," she says.

"I'm not sure how talking about them would work though," I state.

"Are there other types of treatment you think would work for you?"

"I guess there are 3 options? Medicines, talking to a therapist, or a frontal lobotomy. Of the three, I'd really only consider talking to a therapist. But it doesn't feel like talking would be helpful."

"You don't believe talking is helpful?" she asks me

"I guess I see it being helpful to others, but not to me."

"If it works for others, why wouldn't it work for you?"

"Maybe I'm just afraid of it. Afraid to feel those feelings."

"You know I sing in the church and our choir is filled with people with varying degrees of vocal ability and confidence. The most confident singers are not always the best singers, and the best singers are not always the most confident. Some of the most beautiful voices I've ever heard come from people who are afraid to sing. I'd think it would be such a shame to let the most beautiful voice go unheard just because of fear. Fear is nothing but a feeling and feelings are fleeting. They come and go with the wind. Yes, I know they can feel strong, but you feel them and they blow away. I think it would be wonderful to watch you release the bind that your worrying seems to have on you."

"Feelings are fleeting?"

"Can't hold on to them even if you try."

"What do you mean?"

"Do you remember a time when you laughed really hard? At the time, whatever made you laugh, it made your whole body laugh. It's a wonderful feeling, and then it goes away. It's the same with any feeling. You feel it fully in that moment, and then it goes away. God didn't make us so that we could hold onto any intense feeling for long. You feel them and then they fade a bit, or entirely."

I think about saying, "Love you" to that busboy. At the time, I thought I would die with embarrassment. I couldn't even breathe. But Miss Bonnie is right. Even though that was dreadfully embarrassing, and still is kind of embarrassing, I don't feel the same amount of embarrassment anymore. I'm not laughing about it, but I'm also not dying because I accidentally chose the wrong phrase in a diner.

"I guess you're kinda right about that."

"I remember the first time I rode a bike. I was so scared of falling, but each time I rode, it got easier. One day it was just easy. If I hadn't faced that fear that first time, I would've missed out on years of riding around with my friends when I was a young girl. Perhaps consider talking with someone about your worrying. If you find it helpful, great. Keep going. If not, you could stop going."

"Well, Miss Bonnie. Thank you for talking to me. It was really nice of you. I hope you have a nice evening."

"Best of luck to you dear," she says.

I walk back to my house and wonder if talking with someone could help me. I consider what she said about feelings being fleeting. You feel them and then they blow on in the wind. Other people actually seem to act just like that. They have their big feelings and then they move on. For me, the feelings seem so big that I don't think I can handle them, and then time passes and things just keep moving on anyway. Feelings aren't as intense over time. I don't want to be like my mom and fuss over every little thing. Maybe if I talk about things with someone, I could learn ways to make each day a little less intense. I think I'll look into scheduling an appointment.

## AN ANALYSIS OF EMILY'S STORY

This story portrays Emily living with anxiety. Anxiety disorders are characterized by excessive worry, panic, and fear. In order to be diagnosed with an anxiety disorder, the worry and fear need to interfere with key areas of functioning (school, work, family). We can see this in Emily's story when she resists pursuing an advanced degree because she is afraid of feedback. She has difficulty interacting socially (at the coffee shop), worries about being seen in public (getting mail from her mailbox), refuses to eat at her favorite diner (for fear of seeing a busboy), and catastrophizes (her cancer scare).

Treatments for anxiety disorders exist and have a strong evidence base, including cognitive-behavioral treatments described in this book. With treatment, Emily could learn to slow down her automatic thoughts and challenge or reconsider whether her thoughts are true. We see this demonstrated in Emily's story when she talks to her neighbor Bonnie. Bonnie helped her to consider how she experiences feelings.

For example, when Emily said "I love you" instead of "thank you" to the busboy, she was mortified. Bonnie talked with her about the brain's inability to hold onto strong emotions. You can't hold on to that intense feeling for very long, even if you want to. Bonnie helped her to see that even though she was mortified in that moment, she no longer feels the same intensity of mortification. Feelings, even strong feelings, are hard to hold on to. Thus, even though it was embarrassing at the time, it won't always feel embarrassing. Might even be a funny story at some point in her life. Emily realized that even though she felt uncomfortable in the moment, that discomfort can't retain its power.

Emily changed her perspective on seeking help. When Bonnie asked Emily if she ever considered seeking help, Emily replied that she didn't think it would work for her. Emily's initial thoughts about treatment were:

| INITIAL THOUGHTS |
| --- |
| "If my mother couldn't fix me, nothing could." |
| "It won't work for me." |
| "I'm not sure how talking to someone can help." |

| INITIAL FEELINGS |
| --- |
| Anxious |
| Nervous |
| Avoidant |
| **INITIAL BEHAVIORS** |
| Avoid uncomfortable situations |

During their talk, Emily was able to reconsider these thoughts and change them.

| NEW THOUGHTS |
| --- |
| "My mother might have been the one to make me like this." |
| "I would like to learn strategies to manage panic." |
| "Feelings are fleeting. They don't last forever." |
| **NEW FEELINGS** |
| Hopeful |
| Nervous |
| **NEW BEHAVIORS** |
| Schedule an appointment to work with a therapist on panic attacks |

# WORKING THROUGH RESISTANCE TO TREATMENT

Some people indicate that the reason they will not go to treatment is because **they don't believe that treatment works.** When someone says that they don't believe treatment works, there are ways to have a discussion with them on this belief.

The next section of this chapter will focus on how to have conversations with individuals who indicate that treatment for mental health or substance use treatment won't work; and ways you can help someone reconsider these thoughts so they are more likely to consider getting help.

Someone who believes that treatment won't work will say things like:

- "It won't work."
- "There is no point, nothing will work."

If someone in your life is refusing treatment and saying these thoughts, consider asking the following four questions to get them to reconsider these thoughts:

1. What is "treatment?"
2. What are your treatment options?
3. What types of treatment work for a particular condition?
4. What are your treatment goals?

Once you consider these four factors, it may be easier to list out potential evidence-based options that would work for any specific individual.

## "WHAT IS TREATMENT?"

To have an effective conversation with someone about mental health or substance use treatment, you have to understand their definition of treatment. Some people might believe that all treatments require inpatient hospitalization, or that they would be required to attend AA meetings, or that therapy involves sitting on a couch while a therapist asks you about your childhood. Perceptions about what treatment is influence whether someone is willing to consider going to treatment (or seeking help). *Ask them what they think treatment is.* What is "treatment" to them?

## WHAT ARE YOUR TREATMENT OPTIONS?

Once they describe what they think treatment is, **ask them what they think might work for them.** They may say they think retirement would help. Or winning millions of dollars in the lottery. These "treatments" could, in fact, be helpful; however, they might not be readily accessible or long-term fixes. In the event that their preferred "treatment" is not available, ask them to consider what they think would be helpful to them in terms of mental health and substance use treatment.

Some individuals may indicate that they would like to talk to a counselor one-on-one. Other individuals might prefer a medication to manage their symptoms. Others will state that they think they would benefit if they could talk to others that are in a similar situation. Whatever their preferences are, these options are probably available to them. Websites such as Psychology Today or NIMH (National Institute of Mental Health) or NAMI

(National Alliance for Mental Illness) may be helpful places to search for available treatment options. Please see Chapter 11 for additional resources.

## TREATMENT EFFECTIVENESS

While it's important to understand what someone thinks will work for them, it's also a good idea to assess how well the identified treatment works, in general. Data on treatment for mental health and substance use disorders are available. The National Institute for Health houses data on treatment effectiveness for specific conditions and is a good place to start for accurate and reliable data.

Try asking them if their preferred treatment works. Here are some general tips:

- **In general, interventions for mental health and substance use disorders work.** It is best to match the gold standard treatment for that condition, but any start of treatment can start the journey towards better health.
- **Certain conditions are difficult to treat.**
- **Therapists follow therapeutic protocols** and should provide the name and process for the standardized treatments they provide.
- **Therapeutic interventions tend to last around 8-12 weeks.** For more severe and serious conditions, intervention may last slightly longer, but therapy should not last for years.

- **If you are with a therapist for more than 3-4 months, progress may not occur.** You could begin the search for a new therapist or discuss the lack of progress with the provider you are seeing.

- **It is okay to shop around and find a provider that is a good fit.** Psychologytoday.com is an excellent resource for "shopping."

- **Some medications require time.** This is biochemical. Trust the process if you have been prescribed a medication for it to take effect.

## TREATMENT GOALS

Finally (and importantly), **ask them what they would like to work on in treatment.** It may seem obvious that someone is struggling with PTSD, for example, but if you ask them what they would like help with, they may say that they would really like to get help for their insomnia. Start where they are. If the most pressing issue to them is insomnia, start with the insomnia. Perhaps once they have less sleep disturbance, they would be willing to work on the issues causing the sleep disturbance. Encourage them to outline their own treatment goals. For example:

Mike has been performing poorly at work, is not sleeping well, is gaining weight, and is isolating. His family notices that Mike seems down and is not participating in family activities as he normally does. His wife asks Mike to consider getting help because he seems depressed, and depression runs in his family. Mike indicates that he does not wish to get help for depression but would be willing to speak with a doctor about weight gain. His wife asks if there is anything else he'd like to work on with a doctor, and Mike admits that he is also having trouble sleeping and feels down.

Identifying initial treatment goals is a good step towards treatment. Goals may change over time, and that's okay.

Initial treatment goals for Mike include:

1. Learn strategies to control weight gain

2. Learn strategies to sleep better

3. Learn strategies to improve mood/energy

Identify what goals an individual would like to work on in treatment. Goals may change over time.

## PUTTING IT ALL TOGETHER

Putting it all together, let's say that Mike's wife asked these four questions to Mike. Mike's responses are indicated below. These helped him outline whether or not he would seek help and what kind of help he wanted.

| MIKE | |
|---|---|
| **What is Treatment?** | Mike believes that treatment for depression is sitting on a couch talking about childhood. He is not interested in talking about the past. |
| **Treatment Options** | Mike believes there are two treatment options:<br><br>• Counseling<br><br>• Medications |
| **Does the Treatment Work?** | • Mike understands that counseling works for people, but he is not interested because he doesn't want to talk about his past<br><br>• Would only be interested in learning concrete sleep and eating strategies<br><br>• Understands that medications work to treat depression |
| **Goals in Treatment** | • Mike's goals are:<br>• Learn strategies to control weight<br>• Learn strategies to sleep better<br>• Learn strategies to improve mood/ energy |

While outlining his goals with his wife, Mike recognized that he might do best with a combination of medication and short-term counseling. He believes the medications could help his brain, while short-term counseling could help the way he approaches each day. He would like to develop better coping strategies but does not wish to talk to anyone about the past.

Going back to Emily, the following chart shows Emily's responses to these four questions regarding getting help. Asking these four questions can help a person who believes that treatment would not work for them to think through their choice about getting help more fully.

| EMILY | |
| --- | --- |
| **What is Treatment?** | Emily believes that treatment is talking to a psychologist. She isn't sure how talking will help her. |
| **Treatment Options** | Emily indicated three options for getting help:<br><br>• Medications<br>• Talking to a therapist<br>• Frontal lobotomy |
| **Does the Treatment Work?** | • Medications may work but she does not want to take them.<br>• She will research the evidence on talk therapy. She believes it works for some people.<br>• Frontal lobotomy is not an option. |
| **Goals in Treatment** | Emily indicated that she had two things that she would like to work on in treatment:<br><br>• Anxiety<br>• Panic attacks |

**Tips & Suggestions**

- Ask any or all of these four questions.
- Questions can be in any particular order.
- Be considerate and without judgement.

# KEY SUMMARY POINTS

The main idea of this chapter is that people don't seek help because they don't believe that treatment will work. Talking through treatment and treatment options may help them decide which treatment would work best for them.

Four questions to consider when discussing this type of thought:

1. Have them define what treatment is to them.
2. Identify treatment options.
3. Identify treatment effectiveness.
4. Identify treatment goals.

## DECISION TREE

**Prompt:** "I don't want to consider treatment because treatment won't work."

What are your thoughts about getting help?

"Treatment won't work."

**Treatment Definition:** Clarify their definition of what treatment is and allow them to think through what it means to them.

**Treatment Options:** Consult websites for options (medications, therapies, AA/NA, self-help).

**Treatment Effectiveness:** Consult websites for data on treatment effectiveness.

**Treatment Goals:** What do they want to focus on in treatment?

# CHAPTER 4

# "I DON'T WANT 'THAT' TYPE OF TREATMENT"

**T**HIS CHAPTER HIGHLIGHTS how to talk to someone who isn't seeking help because they believe that they only want a certain type of treatment. The chapter starts with the story of Jorge to illustrate an example of how to talk to someone who believes this thought. The chapter ends with suggestions for how to change someone's mind when they believe this thought.

## JORGE'S STORY: A CASE STUDY

**Crisis Line Responder:** How can I help you today?

**Jorge:** (*crying*) Please tell her I love her.

**Responder:** Sir?

**Jorge:** She is better off without me.

**Responder:** Sir? Are you thinking of hurting yourself?

**Jorge:** I am a burden. Nothing is working out.

**Responder:** What is not working out?

**Jorge:** It is all darkness now.

**Responder:** What do you mean by darkness? What is the darkness?

I just wanted to take care of my family. My parents sacrificed so much for me. They arranged their lives around my travel schedule. They cheered for me. Every game mattered, from Little League on up to the minor leagues. Mom made a special meal before the big games. Has been doing it since I was 7 years old and just starting in Little League. She said it was a magic meal and would help me play well. I think it was a magic meal, because it always worked. Until I got hurt.

It's over now. I can't play anymore. Had to medically retire before I hit the show. I rehabbed and tried everything to stay in the game, but doc says it's over for me. I was hopeful, but nothing worked. I had everything. Everything. And I loved it. I loved every day of my life. Until now. I played baseball, in the minors working my way up to the show. A beautiful wife. The woman of my dreams. And a beautiful, innocent, sweet daughter. A daughter! I have a family that I love and a God who loves me. And it's all gone now. Now all I see is dark.

We rehabbed my injury. It was going to take time to get better, but we believed I'd be back. Maybe even better than before because I was working so hard. Things were going to be okay. It hurt and I was frustrated, but I was on my way back. My dream was to play center field on a Major League Baseball team. It's the only dream I've ever had. I love baseball. Love the sound of the ball hitting the bat, the umpire calling the count, the fans in the stands. Love my teammates and the laughs and even the long bus rides home after the game when most of us are trying to sleep but a few cut up and mess around. But man, I really love the Star-Spangled Banner before each game. The guys call me Marquee because when that song starts, I close my eyes, put my hat on my heart, put down my head, and sing along. That song signaled the start of a new game. We were about to play.

Now, I don't know who I am anymore.

I am lost.

My daughter is three. She is so beautiful.

**Responder:** Sir? Are you there, sir? Can you talk to me?

**Jorge:** I was supposed to take care of my family. I am failing.

**Responder:** Tell me about your family.

My wife is stunning. The sun, the moon, and the stars aligned when she agreed to marry me. I vowed to take care of her forever. Our families and my teammates all flew in for the wedding and it was a perfect day. I am shattered that I can't take care of her the way I meant to. I thought if I kept moving forward, I'd find my way, but nothing is working. She worries and tells me I can work through this. I am trying, but I can't. After spending six months rehabbing, docs said I could never play the sport I love again. My father is the head of maintenance at an apartment complex, and he got me a job working with him. The pay is okay, and I am still strong. I can learn anything and eager to prove my worth.

**Responder:** Sir?

**Jorge:** My parents are wonderful.

My father is the head of maintenance at an apartment complex and my mom is a nursery school teacher. My mother loves children. Every year in their backyard they have an Easter Egg hunt. Many children come, and she loves them all. She spends the entire year picking out prizes. She stuffs what must be a thousand plastic eggs with little candies, but in 10 of them she places a piece of paper with the word PRIZE on it. She works so hard to make sure that whoever finds a PRIZE egg will be awarded something special. She'll pick out prizes appropriate for any child at any age and when the hunt is over, she loves to hand out their special prize gift.

I am failing.

Working as a maintenance man at an apartment complex is not the same as being a professional baseball player. But it is honest work and does good for people, so I was okay in my new role. I am limited in terms of my injury but strong enough to work through it. My father placed Jimmy in charge of teaching me the ropes. Jimmy has worked with my dad for the past 22 years and is a good employee. He is small in stature, not strong, and only has one eye. The first year he worked for my father, a rock flew out from under the mower and hit him straight in the face. He is a black man but chose a green eye for his replacement. He's proud of his replacement eyeball, but it can take a bit of getting used to looking at someone with one brown eye and one green eye. Jimmy is family and I've known him for forever. He is a hard worker.

One day, we had to dig up the water line to locate a leak and Jimmy accidentally slammed a shovel on top of my foot. Hit right along the quick of the big toenail. My toenail turned black, and I eventually lost it. It hurt so bad, had to hobble around for weeks. I don't think Jimmy has great depth perception with only one eye.

Maintenance is harder than I thought. Moving huge appliances up and down stairs, sometimes onto the roof, it's a wonder any of us survive. One time, I had to move a fridge up these stairs where I couldn't use a dolly. The turns were too tight and I couldn't make the corners. I literally had to pick it up and move it with my arms and hands one step at a time. And some of the calls we get from residents! Most are nice people, but you never know what they might ask you to do.

My father never complained so I didn't know exactly what I was getting into. After the call from the resident in Apt 42, I get it now. She called and indicated she had a problem with her toilet and then sat behind me to talk while I cut up the biggest poo I've ever seen in my life just to flush her toilet. She talked about dinner and her children like there was nothing unusual going on. It's not every day I have to manipulate poo. And I was a baseball player hanging out with athletes so I've seen a lot, but that was by far the worst.

Having an injury, losing my dream of playing baseball, a crushed toenail, moving enormous appliances, and toilet troubles all bothered me, but I promised myself that I would keep on. For my family. My parents and my wife and my daughter.

My daughter. Isabella. She's 3 years old. When I played ball, I would get home most nights anytime between midnight and 3am. Then I would sleep until noon, get up and go back to the field. Now, I have a regular job but still can get home late. And exhausted. And hot. Last night, I was so tired, too tired to eat, she was already in bed. I sat in her rocking chair and watched her sleep. She hardly moved. She looked so peaceful. I vowed again that her life would be okay.

I haven't been sleeping much this past week because of the projects at work. We are replacing many of the AC units and it is hot and heavy work. It's August in Florida so the weather is brutal for this job, but the units are old and failing. My father and Jimmy help as much as they can but they are older and not as strong. Another guy, Dwayne, and I do much of the heavy lifting, but with the heat and humidity, it's tough and we want to collapse. We are drenched with sweat. This is more of a workout than anything I did in professional sports. But I will not complain even if my muscles are twitching and cramping in dehydration.

Tonight though. I broke my code. I have become someone I do not recognize. I am exhausted from many nights of sleep deprivation while we get this job done and it's hot beyond belief. But that is no excuse for what I did. Many of the tenants talk with us about their faltering air conditioning units. They know the units are old and need to be replaced, so for the most part, the tenants have been patient and encouraging of our loud, long, laborious replacement project. There are a few tenants; however, who berate rather than encourage. They tell us it took too long and ask when we will be done. Harriet in apartment 28 glared at me today and said, "About time you all get off your asses and fix something around here." It hurts me to hear these comments. My father has been dedicated to this place for so long and works hard to make sure things are in working order. It is true that the units are old and need replacing but he was only allowed to replace them after years of encouraging the owners and the board to do so.

So today, I was up in the attic of one of the units where it must have been 130+ degrees. As I was climbing down the ladder, Sheila accosted me. There is always a Sheila. The problem person. The last person you want to talk to when you are sleep deprived, hot, and frustrated. She often complains and yells at staff. Climbing down the ladder, sweat pouring off me, wanting nothing more than to jump into a cold tub of water, I hear her say, "YOU!" I close my eyes to take a moment to find my center and take a deep breath. Just like I would when I was up to bat against a talented pitcher. Maintaining as much composure as I possibly can, I ask, "How are you today, Sheila?"

"Do you have any idea how hot it is in my apartment?" She asks.

"Yes, ma'am. We are replacing the units as fast as we can," I tell her.

"I can't sleep, I can't cook, I can't live like this! My plants are wilting in my apartment. Are you going to pay to replace my plants? I feel like you are deliberately doing my apartment last!"

I do not reply, mostly because I feel queasy and dizzy from being in the hot attic but also because it is difficult to understand what she is saying about her plants.

"BOY, I AM TALKING TO YOU!" she screams at me.

To my credit, I turn to walk away but she follows me screaming something or other. I can't really understand what she is saying as I feel desperate to get away, but I snap to when I hear her shout, "That Carlos is HORRIBLE at keeping up with ANYTHING around here."

Carlos is my father and God forgive me, but I am used to being cheered at work. Yes, baseball players have the occasional slump, and people can get nasty about those, but it comes with a strong fan base that encourages us. We have fans and snacks. Maintenance men do not have fans. Or snacks. They hear complaints.

"God as my witness, WE WILL REPLACE YOUR FUCKING UNIT LAST! It wouldn't matter if we replaced it first though because your soul is so EVIL, you will rot in hell wherever you are!" I yell as I walk away.

I hear her shriek and yell something about me losing my job. I am not a violent man, but I thank the Lord Jesus above I did not throw her down the hallway. I walked straight to my car and spent the last 20 minutes in the air conditioning trying to regain my composure.

This is where I am when I realize I am lost. I don't know who I am anymore. I am exhausted and unsure if I can continue. I don't wish my wife and child to see me like this. They are better off without the lost and angry man I have become. I don't talk to people like that. It's not what I do. It's not who I am. I should leave them before I do anything worse or sink deeper into this hole. I want them to know I love them and that they do not have to be burdened by my failings. I can end all of this suffering by taking the gun out of the glove compartment.

This is when I called the crisis line.

**Responder:** Sir? Are you still there? Can you tell me your name?

**Jorge:** My name is Jorge.

**Responder:** Hi Jorge. Can you tell me a little about yourself?

**Jorge:** I am not a violent man. I don't speak to people like I did today.

**Responder:** Will you talk to me about it?

**Jorge:** I yelled at a tenant. I was very rude.

**Responder:** You were not yourself today? What was going on for you?

**Jorge:** I haven't been sleeping. I got hurt and had to change jobs recently. Change my whole life. I don't know who I am anymore. I don't know if I can do this anymore.

**Responder:** How bad has your sleep been this past week?

**Jorge:** We have a big project at work. By the time I get home, I sleep for an hour or two before I get up to go back to work. It's so hot during the day. It's better to get some of the work done when the sun is not out. But we can only do so much because we don't want to disturb the tenants at night. The rest we do in the heat of the day.

**Responder:** So, this past week, you have only been getting a couple of hours of sleep each night and you've been working outside in the Florida heat during the day?

**Jorge:** Yes ma'am.

**Responder:** Well that sounds like a tough assignment. Maybe anyone would be agitated and feel like they've lost their way?

**Jorge:** I should not complain.

**Responder:** You said you had to change jobs recently?

**Jorge:** Yes. I got hurt playing baseball and I can't play anymore.

**Responder:** That must have been hard.

**Jorge:** Yes. Baseball was my dream. But I still need to take care of my family so I took a job working with my father.

**Responder:** And that is where you yelled at the tenant?

**Jorge:** Yes. I brought shame to my family.

**Responder:** You brought shame to your family?

**Jorge:** Yes.

**Responder:** What does this mean in your family? To bring shame?

**Jorge:** I have disappointed them. I never want to disappoint them. I was set to play major league baseball and take care of them forever. That is over, so I work maintenance with my father and I messed up today. I can move refrigerators and AC units and not complain though it is hot, heavy, grueling work. We don't sleep because it's too hot to work during the day and we have to get these jobs completed. I am used to people cheering for me. Now people are mean and demanding. I am struggling. I don't know how to move forward.

**Responder:** You were thinking of harming yourself when you called?

My daughter. We took her to the emergency room once. She was very sick with a cold and not able to breathe. I was scared watching her struggle to breathe. My wife and I rushed to the doctor. The doctors were good during the examination and gave her oxygen. I remember thinking, "Please God. Let her be okay. I'll take the suffering. Bring anything to me, but please let her breathe. Let me be the sick one. Not her.

**Jorge:** I just want my family to be okay. For my daughter to be okay. She might be better off without me.

**Responder:** I know that you are having a hard time today and it's difficult to think straight when you are sleep deprived, but I want you to understand that when children lose a parent to suicide, they often do not feel relieved of a burden. They often blame themselves and wonder why they weren't worth living for.

**Jorge:** (crying) She is worth everything.

**Responder:** Have you thought about getting help?

**Jorge:** What do you mean help?

**Responder:** Talking to someone about what is going on for you? Sounds like you have had major changes lately and you are sleep deprived.

**Jorge:** Like a doctor?

**Responder:** Yes, like a doctor.

**Jorge:** No. I don't want to talk to a doctor. They would just give me a medicine and I don't want to take a medicine. A medicine will not solve this.

**Responder:** Okay, I understand. You don't want to take a medicine. There are other doctors you could talk to, for example, a therapist. A therapist could help you work through all the changes that have happened to you recently.

**Jorge:** Oh. A therapist. Well, I hadn't thought of that. I could talk to a therapist.

**Responder:** It sounds like you love your family and had a tough moment. Can we get you some options for therapists you can work with?

**Jorge:** Yes, ma'am. Yes, thank you. I had not thought about calling a therapist, but I think it would be good to talk to someone.

## AN ANALYSIS OF JORGE'S STORY

While Jorge has a strong work ethic and love for his family, he experienced some notable challenges. He was forced to retire from a promising baseball career because of an injury and his new job was physically demanding. The new job was not only physically grueling in very hot conditions, but Jorge was sleep deprived. The sleep deprivation and physical demands disrupted Jorge's equilibrium resulting in personality changes. This, on top of his loss of a promising career, impacted Jorge's emotional well-being and he lashed out at a tenant at his job.

Jorge may benefit from working with a mental health professional to talk about his major life changes and to potentially establish healthy boundaries and coping skills (such as prioritizing sleep).

Jorge was able to change his thoughts about seeking help during his call with the crisis line responder. When the responder asked Jorge his thoughts on seeking help, Jorge initially rejected the idea of talking with a doctor because he believed they would only prescribe him a medication and he didn't believe a medication would help. He did; however, embrace the idea of talking to a therapist and liked the idea of talking to someone about all the changes he had been experiencing. Jorge's initial thoughts about treatment were:

| INITIAL THOUGHTS |
| --- |
| "I don't want a medicine." |
| **INITIAL FEELINGS** |
| Agitated, depressed, hopeless |
| **INITIAL BEHAVIORS** |
| Considers hurting self, calls crisis line |

After the discussion with the responder on seeking help, Jorge changed his thoughts to:

| NEW THOUGHTS |
| --- |
| "I don't want a medicine, but I would like to work with a therapist." |
| **NEW FEELINGS** |
| Needs to take care of family |
| **NEW BEHAVIORS** |
| Schedule an appointment with a therapist. |

# WORKING THROUGH RESISTANCE TO TREATMENT

Some people indicate that the reason they will not go to treatment is because they do not want a particular type of treatment. This is the **most prevalent** reason why people indicate they are not seeking help. It's also the easiest one to change. When someone says that they don't want a particular type of treatment, let them know they have choices in treatment and won't be forced to do any particular one.

The next section of this chapter will focus on how to have conversations with individuals who indicate that they don't want a particular mental health or substance use treatment; and ways you can help someone reconsider these thoughts so they are more likely to consider getting help.

Someone who believes that they don't want a particular treatment will say things like:

- I don't want to be in a group like AA.
- I don't want to be hospitalized.
- I don't want medication.
- I don't want therapy.

If someone in your life is refusing treatment and saying these thoughts, there are a variety of ways to have a discussion with them to get them to reconsider these thoughts, but the best options are to **acknowledge what they don't want** and **investigate other options.**

## ACKNOWLEDGE WHAT THEY *DON'T* WANT

- If someone states they don't want a particular type of treatment, that's okay.

- If someone says, "I don't want medicine," you can say, "I hear you. You don't want to take medicine."

- If someone says, "I don't want to go to AA," you can say, "I hear you. You don't want to go to AA."

- If someone says, "I don't want therapy," you can say, "I hear you. You don't want to go to therapy."

For most mental health and substance use conditions, there are a variety of treatment options. In general, what will work best for a particular person is a combination of the gold standard, evidence-based treatment *and* what they believe will work best for them. It is perfectly reasonable to have a preferred treatment.

In Jorge's story, the responder asked Jorge his thoughts on getting help and Jorge responded that he did not want to see a doctor because a doctor would prescribe a medication, and he didn't believe that a medication would be helpful. The responder acknowledged that Jorge did not want to be prescribed medication.

## INVESTIGATE OTHER OPTIONS

If someone indicates that there is a particular type of treatment that does not work for them, ask them if there is a treatment they think might work better for them. Investigate options. Evidence-based treatment options exist for most mental health and substance use conditions. (To find more information on evidence-based treatments, please consult Chapter 10.)

**Encourage them to seek whichever treatment they prefer.** In Jorge's story, the responder does this when they ask if there were other providers Jorge might be interested in seeing, like a therapist. Jorge agreed that seeing a therapist and talking to someone might be helpful.

## KEY SUMMARY POINTS

The main idea of this chapter is that people don't seek help because they believe if they reach out for help, they will be required to get a certain type of treatment that they don't want. Reassure them that they have options and can choose the treatment they think is the right fit for them.

Strategies to overcome these thoughts include:

1.  Acknowledge what they don't want.

2.  Identify options that they think are a better fit for them.

## DECISION TREE

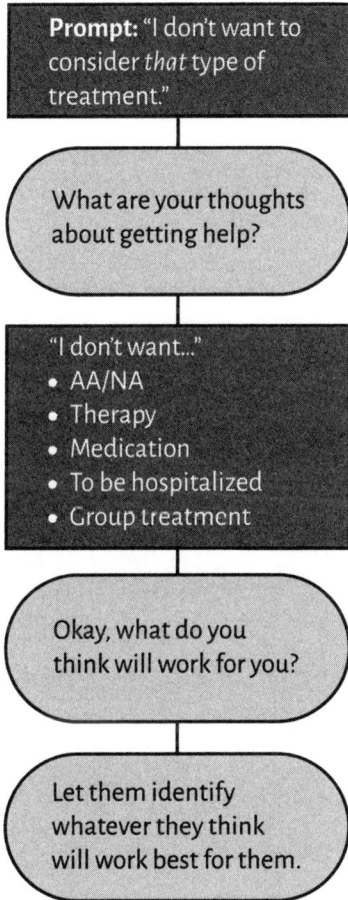

**Prompt:** "I don't want to consider *that* type of treatment."

What are your thoughts about getting help?

"I don't want..."
- AA/NA
- Therapy
- Medication
- To be hospitalized
- Group treatment

Okay, what do you think will work for you?

Let them identify whatever they think will work best for them.

# CHAPTER 5

# "IT'S TOO HARD TO OPEN UP"

**T**HIS CHAPTER HIGHLIGHTS how to talk to someone who isn't seeking help because they believe that it is too hard to open up or treatment will be too intense. The chapter starts with the story of Avery to illustrate an example of how to talk to someone who believes this. The chapter ends with suggestions for how to change someone's mind when they believe this thought.

## AVERY'S STORY: A CASE STUDY

Holidays are when I most want to die. It's hard to be around everyone, seeing their looks of concern, knowing that what is easy for them is so hard for me. They aren't fat like I am. They don't have to work so hard. For me, I have to think about how much I eat all of the time. So, you can imagine how hard holidays are, with everyone eating, laughing, enjoying themselves.

It's different for me.

We are at my aunt's house for Thanksgiving. I have a big family and they are all perfect. Fun, happy, successful, skinny. It's like everything is easy for them. Everything feels hard for me. Even breathing is hard sometimes.

My aunt lives in a huge farmhouse, with extra rooms for all of us. There are a lot of us, as we have a big family, but no one seems to mind being all jammed together. In fact, they love it! I don't want to sound ungrateful because I love them. I love them so much. They are wonderful. It's *me* I don't like.

It started a couple of years ago when one of my friends lost weight. She looked great. She didn't even need to lose weight, but everyone was really nice to her afterwards. She got a lot of compliments. One day another friend was telling her how great she looked after she lost weight and turned to pat me on my stomach. I was so embarrassed. It felt so awkward. I don't know if she was trying to tell me I was fat, but it felt like that was what she was saying. In my head, I could feel her hand rubbing my belly for days. I can still remember what it felt like to have her hand on my belly. It was that moment I decided to stop eating.

I stopped eating breakfast and lunch and would only eat a little for dinner. Breakfast was easy to skip because mornings are crazy at my house with everyone running around getting ready for school and work. I'd tell my mom I was grabbing a protein bar or a yogurt. I wouldn't eat it but would make her think I was. At school, lunch is when kids are hanging out, not necessarily eating and there is a lot of chaos, so it was easy to not eat. A little harder to not eat dinner though because my mom is a great cook. And she sits with us at the table. I would ask for extra veggies and try to eat those but not much else.

This worked for a while, but then my mom started asking me to eat more. And she started to stare at me. It got so awkward that it was even hard to eat my vegetables with her staring at me like that. She'd say things like, "I wish you would eat a little more. I'm worried about you." My dad would say things like, "Leave her alone. She is beautiful."

Recently, I heard them arguing in their bedroom. My parents rarely fight, but that night, I could hear her telling my dad, "I'm worried about her, Andrew! She's skin and bone." My dad said, "Leave her be. She's having a phase all girls have. She'll work through it." My mom said, "This is beyond a phase. She's gone too far, and I'm scared. She doesn't have any energy to do her schoolwork. She's not hanging out with any of her friends. She isolates in her room. She's not eating and she's wasting away!"

"She had chocolate tonight!" my dad says.

"For heaven's sake, that was one Hershey's kiss! She can't exist on a Hershey's kiss! Do you think a Hershey's kiss is going to keep her alive?" My mom screams.

"You're being dramatic. Harassing her isn't going to make her eat."

"Ignore it and she'll *die!*"

"Relax. Girls diet to be thin. It's a teenage girl thing."

"Diet sure, but this is *anorexia*. It's gone too far!"

"What do you want to do? Force her to eat??"

"YES! That is *exactly* what I want to do. I want her to get help and I want her to EAT!"

Dad sighs loud enough that I can hear him and says, "I don't think you need to be so worried. She eats every day. We see her eat every day."

"Not enough. She is not eating enough."

"She'll work through this, and it'll pass soon enough."

"BECAUSE SHE WILL BE DEAD!" I can hear her crying. Sobbing really. And I can tell my dad walked over to hold her while she cries. My dad doesn't like for people to cry or be emotional.

I don't like my mom to be upset either. I feel really bad that I've made her cry. I love my parents and it stresses me that they are fighting over me. I don't want to cause them any pain. I can't eat though. I'm still fat.

The day after my parents fight, I ask my mom to buy me some trail mix. She knows I like trail mix and used to buy it for me all the time a couple of years ago. I ask for it in the morning before school. After school, the trail mix is in the pantry. I make sure that she sees me taking some out of the bag and put it in a bowl. Then I go outside and sit.

She seems happy to see me grab food, even if it is just a little bit of trail mix. I get the sense that she wants to say something to me, but she doesn't. I sit in the backyard and watch the chipmunks and squirrels run around the yard. I envy them. They seem happy and free. The chipmunks are so cute. One gets kinda close to me so I throw a nut to him. He picks it up and stuffs it in his cheek. He looks funny with a nut stuffed in one side of the cheek, so I throw the rest of the nuts to him. He stuffs all of them in his mouth and then runs off. Even a chipmunk can do what is so hard for me. My mom doesn't need to know that I gave most of the trail mix away. I just wanted her to feel happy for a minute.

Which leads us back to Thanksgiving Day at my aunt's house. Part of me didn't even want to go, because I know people will stare at me, but I love seeing my family. I have a lot of cousins and they are fun and crazy. There are about 40 people at Thanksgiving this year and the big story of the day is my cousin Tori. She smelled so bad. When my aunt opened the door to greet her, she screamed and said, "UGH! What is that smell?"

Tori says, "Oh my god, you will not believe what happened to me this morning! I startled a skunk in my yard, and it sprayed me!"

"Tori! Why didn't you change your clothes?"

"I DID! I showered and changed my clothes!"

"Well, it smells awful!"

Tori looks pitiful, which is not like her. She's usually the fun one who makes everyone happy but it's hard to look at her because she really does smell bad. She says, "Should I just leave?"

"Of course not! It's Thanksgiving and you have to be here. You may need to eat out in the barn though." Again, a pained look crosses Tori's face.

Tori is the cousin who is always off on an adventure. She has lived all over the States, visited countries all over the world advocating for human rights, goes on adventures like rock climbing and sky diving. She's beautiful and never has to worry about her weight. She's got a million friends, and everyone loves her. Well, everyone I guess except for that skunk.

After some debate, the family decides that Tori needs to take a bath in tomato juice so Uncle Harold goes to the store and buys as much tomato juice as he can. She is sitting in the tub right now soaking in it. I feel bad for her, but I'm also glad the attention is on her and her skunk versus me and food.

I knock on the bathroom door to visit with Tori.

"Tori? Can I come in?"

"Avery, come talk to me! Distract me from the fact that I'm in a tub of tomato juice. My mom gave me *her* clothes to put on and she threw mine in the trash!" she says as she laughs. She is pouring cups of tomato juice over the top of her head to get the skunk smell out of her hair. I can't imagine how embarrassing this is, but she seems like she's going with the flow. "This will be another holiday to remember. Sprayed by a skunk, have the entire family run away from me, bathe in tomato juice, wear my mom's clothes, banished to the barn to eat by myself. It's a perfect Thanksgiving! I bet when we take group photos later, there will be two. One of the entire family and one of me sitting by myself in the barn!"

"You'll never be banished. Everyone wants you here."

"Remember that Christmas when we dressed up like we were living back in the 1930's?"

"The skits were so funny."

"Yeah, they were. So, talk to me. How come you're hiding in here with me?"

"Just wanted to make sure you're okay."

"Are *you* okay?"

"Me? Yeah, I'm okay."

"Yeah? I'm worried about you. You sure you're okay?"

I'm not sure what to say. I feel awkward with her looking at me and nothing is coming to mind to answer her. I feel this way a lot. Uncomfortable. I don't know how I think (or feel) about anything. I thought losing weight would help me feel confident, but it hasn't. I still feel confused. And lost. Everyone seems to know how to act and what to say, but I don't.

While we sit there, we can hear the family talking and laughing. There are so many voices, it's hard to follow any one of them. You can identify someone's voice every once in a while, but can't keep track of any one conversation. There is laughter though. I hear people laughing.

"Avery? Have you ever thought about getting help?"

"Help? What do you mean?"

"Yes, help. As in a therapist."

"Therapist?"

"Yes. A therapist. Come on, Avery. It's been about a year now that you've been losing weight and you are so thin. I'm worried about you."

"I don't want to go to a therapist. No. I wouldn't know what to say. It would be too uncomfortable and talking would just be really intense."

"Maybe that's why you work with a professional though? To help figure out how you're feeling and be able to talk about it?"

"I don't know. My dad says this a phase and if we just leave it alone, it'll all be okay."

"Do you feel okay? Do you feel like you're going to be okay if you just leave it alone?"

I have no answer for that. I don't feel okay. It feels like I'm never going to feel okay. It's all just so confusing. All I know is that I don't want anyone mad at me. They seem more worried than mad, but that's not any better than if they were mad at me!

Still, the idea of talking to a professional does not sound good. I can't imagine how hard it would be. When I try to find words to describe what's going on for me, it seems like the words disappear or something. I can't grab anything. I don't know what to say or do and having someone stare at me and wait for me to explain would be awful.

"You said that talking with someone would be intense. What did you mean by that?"

"Well, you know. Intense. Like it would be hard to talk. I'm not sure I'd be able to do it."

"It would be hard to talk about things?"

"Yeah. I can't explain how hard things are for me."

"What kinds of things are hard? Are things okay at school? At home?"

"Well, yes. It's nothing like that. School is fine and I love my parents. It's me. I just don't know how I feel. About anything. I feel lost. It used to be the easiest thing in the world to sit down at the dinner table with my family and now it's the worst thing."

"What makes it the worst thing?"

"Because my mom stares at me and I know I'm making her feel sad."

"Have you talked to her about that?"

"NO! It would be too hard to talk to her."

"Avery, I've known your mom a long time and she's really easy to talk to. Maybe it would feel better if you talked to her directly about how you are feeling. Or maybe even just tell her that you're not sure how you're feeling or how to explain it. We all go through that as teenagers. High school sucks, but things get better. Easier."

"Were you uncomfortable as a teenager?"

"YES! Ha. My mom could tell you stories. But, yes. I was uncomfortable and unsure of myself and didn't feel like I understood much."

"That's how I feel."

"So maybe you're a normal 18-year-old teenager who started focusing on dieting instead of trying to figure it out. Might be good to talk to your mom and a therapist. It can't hurt, can it?"

"Yes. It could hurt to talk."

"Ha ha ha. Okay, so maybe it hurts the first time you sit down and tell someone how you're feeling, but it will get easier. It gets easier and honestly; it just feels better to talk to someone when you're feeling unsure. Has it been hard to talk to me?"

"Well, no. But you're sitting in a bathtub with tomato juice running down your face because you got sprayed with a skunk."

"Fair point. You said it hurts to talk. Did something happen to you that you don't want to talk about?"

"Well, no. It just hurts to feel things. I want to push bad feelings away."

"Well okay, I can understand that you want to push bad feelings away and not deal with them, but they are just feelings. They pass. Bad feelings feel bad, but they go away. You can't even hold on to them even if you try. I remember when you were little, you got really upset whenever your parents would drop you off so they could have a night out. Do you remember that?"

"Yes. I guess I felt like they were leaving me."

"They always came home. Would you have fun when you were with us those evenings?"

"Yes! We would paint and write skits and watch movies!"

"Exactly. Do you remember the pain you felt when they would leave?"

"Well, no. Not really now."

"That's how pain is. It hurts at the time, yes. And it's awful. But it goes away. Feelings are just feelings. You're going to have plenty of feelings throughout your life and it's a good thing to be able to deal with them."

"Ugh. That sounds so uncomfortable."

"What a gift then to learn how to walk through the discomfort and find yourself on the other side."

I don't know how it's so easy for her. "Tori, it would be too much. Too intense to talk to someone about all of this."

"What does that mean? What does it mean that it would be TOO intense to talk to someone?"

"It feels like I would die!"

"It feels like you would die?"

"Yes!"

"Like, seriously? What does it feel like?"

"It feels like I would have a heart attack, or like the blood in my head would just explode!"

"Avery, never in the history of the universe of the world has someone's head exploded because they talked about their thoughts and feelings."

"But it would feel that way!"

"Okay, but so what? An uncomfortable feeling lasts for a minute or two and then what? You feel a little better? Haven't you ever cried and felt better afterwards? Don't you wonder that if you talked this out with someone, they might give you options and strategies that you hadn't thought about and that maybe you'll be able to move through this a little easier? No one is saying that it will be comfortable, but you're not comfortable now! Might as well try something different!"

She has a point there. I'm not comfortable now. I don't know what to do and maybe I won't die talking to someone.

"Okay. Okay, maybe I can talk to someone, but it has to be someone that I'm comfortable with."

"Okay. Let's look on the psychologytoday.com website and see if we can find someone that you would like to talk to. Okay?"

"Okay."

# AN ANALYSIS OF AVERY'S STORY

Avery has an eating disorder. Eating disorders are characterized by the following symptoms:

- Low body weight, but perceives herself to be fat

- Restriction of food

- Being preoccupied by thoughts of food

- Strong fear of gaining weight

- Low energy

- Difficulty concentrating, confusion

Avery indicated during a discussion with her cousin, Tori, that she is not interested in getting help for her eating behavior because it would be too hard to talk about it, too intense, and she is not sure how to identify or describe her experience. She indicated that she believes that everyone else has an easy time in life but that it is all hard for her.

Avery changed her thoughts about getting help during her talk with Tori. When Tori asked about her thoughts on getting help, Avery said it would be too hard. Tori asked what she meant by "too hard." Avery explained that talking would be so hard that she might die if she talked about what was going on for her (have a heart attack). Tori helped her to consider that even if something feels uncomfortable, or even very uncomfortable, you feel better after. Rarely does anyone die because they attempted to express their thoughts and feelings. They discussed that Avery felt comfortable talking to Tori and maybe could learn to be comfortable talking with other people, including her mother and a therapist.

In the story, we saw Tori support how normal it is to be unsure of oneself as a teenager.

Avery's thoughts started as:

| INITIAL THOUGHTS: |
| --- |
| "It's too hard to open up to someone" |
| "Therapy would be too intense" |
| **INITIAL FEELINGS** |
| Anxious |
| Hopeless |
| Feel stuck |
| **INITIAL BEHAVIORS** |
| Isolate |
| Restrictive eating |
| During the discussion with her cousin, her thoughts changed to: |
| **NEW THOUGHTS** |
| "It is too hard to open up and I don't want to feel my feelings, but I'm feeling them all the time anyway. Might be worth trying something new." |
| "Treatment will be intense, but I'm not going to die from it." |
| **NEW FEELINGS** |
| Anxious |
| Hopeful |
| **NEW BEHAVIORS** |
| Ask mom to help her find a therapist to discuss her eating behaviors. |

# WORKING THROUGH RESISTANCE TO TREATMENT

"It's too hard to open up." "Treatment is too intense."

Some people, like Avery, find it hard to talk about their experiences. It's like asking someone to solve a complex mathematical formula and they don't know how. Thoughts and feelings can be unwieldy, and they can be all over the place. Allowing thoughts and feelings to flow naturally is not always easy or comfortable. Thoughts and feelings are not permanent. They can change, stay the same, evolve, mutate, expand, revert, be revered, and even forgotten. It's important to recognize how you think and feel. Just because you have a thought or a feeling doesn't mean you will die of the thought (or feeling) or that you will always have this thought (or feeling). Life will continue. The sun will come up. Feelings exist and most importantly, even the most painful awful feelings are survivable. Our brains are wired to survive.

The next section of this chapter will focus on the consequences of pushing down feelings; how this impacts thoughts about mental health and substance use disorders and treatment; and ways you can help someone reconsider these thoughts so they are more likely to consider getting help.

Someone struggling to deal with their thoughts and feelings might say things like:

- It's too hard to open up.
- Therapy would be too intense.
- It would be too uncomfortable to talk to someone.

If someone in your life is refusing treatment and expressing these thoughts, there are a variety of ways to have a discussion with them to get them to reconsider these thoughts.

These include discussions about:

1.  Learning to identify and feel the feelings. It's not easy to feel, and it's really not easy to be uncomfortable. However, pushing down feelings makes living in reality difficult. Learn to be okay feeling the discomfort.

2.  Be the mirror. Take an honest look at the situation and the facts.

# IDENTIFY & FEEL THE FEELINGS

Here are some key things to consider when talking with someone who prefers not to feel feelings, particularly negative feelings:

## WHAT PAIN IS BEING AVOIDED?

No one wants to feel bad. Feelings are painful sometimes. People prefer feeling good and prefer pain to go away. This is actually, in some ways, the basis of addiction. Relying on substances helps numb pain so some people use substances to take bad feelings away. The problem is that pain is there for a reason. And it's okay, healthy sometimes, to feel it.

It can be difficult for some people to label or identify feelings beyond good/bad. The spectrum of feelings is broad, and it could be helpful to identify the feeling. Is it guilt, grief, loss, abandonment, rejection? Identifying the underlying feeling is an important step in accepting the reality of the situation.

## WHAT ARE YOU FEELING?

| | |
|---|---|
| Hungry | Abandoned |
| Fearful | Neglected |
| Exhausted | Accepted |
| Angry | Understood |
| Irritated | Ashamed |
| Overstimulated | Proud |
| Scared | Betrayed |
| Good | Trusted |
| Bad | Pained |
| Humbled | Violated |
| Tired | Determined |
| Overwhelmed | Successful |
| Frustrated | Unsure |
| Grateful | Confident |
| Overjoyed | Safe |
| Secure | Rested |
| Alone | Satiated |
| Disconnected | Happy |
| Grief | Calm |
| Rejected | Bored |

| | |
|---|---|
| Annoyed | Graceful |
| Impatient | Awkward |
| Sad | Shy |
| Loved | Satisfied |
| Enraptured | Torn |
| Energized | Uncomfortable |
| Disillusioned | Rattled |
| Disenchanted | Repulsed |
| Unnerved | Needed |
| Discombobulated | Offended |
| Confused | Nice |
| Awed | Naughty |
| Peace | Dirty |
| Serene | Messy |
| Triggered | Funny |
| Activated | Manipulated |
| Amused | Helpless |
| Cheerful | Hopeless |
| Cranky | Valuable |
| Brave | Worthless |
| Anxious | Stressed |
| Defiant | Social |
| Foolish | Restless |
| Forgiving | Cherished |

Identifying the feeling helps clarify the reality of the situation and opens options for making choices on how to move forward. Consider under what circumstances you have experienced each of the above.

## IS THERE A PURPOSE FOR THE PAIN?

Even the most horrible feelings are there with purpose despite how horrible it feels. Sometimes it can feel like you might not survive the *feeling*. But you do. And you learn. An example of this is the feeling of grief. Grief stems from loving someone. When you lose someone you love, it hurts *because* of love. You'd never take away the good feelings you had with the person you loved and lost, and you'd never feel that grief if you didn't love them. So even grief is an opportunity. An opportunity to feel grateful for love. Grateful for the positive memories. Grateful for the experience of having them in your life, even for too short a time.

Other examples of bad feelings being there with purpose include betrayal, rejection, shame, guilt, and violation. You learn from all of these. For the person who was betrayed, you learn trust and discernment. For the person who was rejected, you learn perseverance and options. For the person who felt guilt and/or shame, you learn about consequences and choices moving forward, or motivation for change. For the person who was violated, you learn about safety and self-preservation. Bad feelings are opportunities. If you never let bad feelings fully surface, you miss opportunities to learn and grow.

And yes, I know someone just read the above paragraph and thought that they don't want to learn and grow. Yes, you do.

## AVOIDING THE FEELING KEEPS YOU IN "FEELING PURGATORY"

It takes enormous energy to try and avoid pain. The brain and the body are designed to feel pain for a reason. They *do* remember. In actuality, you don't avoid the feeling at all. The feelings are still there, rising up occasionally, threatening to explode. It takes a lot of effort to force those feelings to stay down. It's like diarrhea. You can try and hold it in for a while, but eventually she's going to explode. It's uncomfortable holding it in and it's uncomfortable letting it out. But eventually, because it came out, you start on the path of feeling better.

Do you want to manage all aspects of life or do you want to crumble at the first sign of pain? For any of us to survive life, and life can be cruel, we have to endure. Being able to endure doesn't mean being able to sidestep pain. It means embracing it (momentarily) and learning how to move *through* it.

Once the feelings are identified, identify ways to express and move through the feeling. Perhaps talking with a friend or a therapist can help express the feelings. Perhaps the feelings can be felt through journaling or art or exercise or dance or music. It's important to identify ways to express the feelings once they are identified.

## BE THE MIRROR & ASSESS THE FACTS

Life is wonderful, but there are situations we would rather not experience. We don't have the option to pick and choose. Some of our experiences are so painful, they can be hard to acknowledge. **It's too hard to admit the truth.** For instance, no one wants their child addicted to drugs and/or alcohol. No one wants a cheating spouse or a gambling addiction or an abusive partner. No one wants to have cancer or to lose someone they love. Life is painful sometimes. None of us get through life without a fair amount of pain. It's unavoidable. Trying to avoid pain doesn't erase the pain (and it takes an enormous amount of energy). Trying to deny it's happening also doesn't erase the pain (because reality has a horrible way of continuing to show up).

## LEARNING TO ACCEPT REALITY

For individuals having a hard time with a situation, it's important to create an atmosphere of truth. Brian, for example, has had his dog Barney for the past nine years. Barney is a golden lab and an important part of Brian's family. Recently, Barney has been vomiting, having seizures, and is lethargic. Brian's wife asks Brian to take the dog to the vet, but Brian insists Barney is okay. He believes that Barney ate something that disagreed with him, and he'll be okay in a couple of days. Because Brian refuses to take the dog to the vet for a medical assessment, Brian's wife takes the dog and discovers that Barney has a brain tumor and likely only has a short time to live. She tells Brian what the vet says, and Brian insists that the vet is wrong and his dog will be okay.

Brian is having difficulty accepting the reality of the situation with his dog. His denial of the dog's physical health does not change the reality of the dog's physical health. Brian prefers to minimize relevant data that points to his dog's poor health and instead focuses on evidence to the contrary. For example, Brian might say things like, "The dog is still drinking water" or "Barney wagged his tail today. See he's not sick!" While it may be true that

Barney drank water and wagged his tail, it's still true that Barney was diagnosed with a fatal tumor. For Brian to begin to accept his dog's reality, he will need to be able to recognize all data (both the positive and negative data).

Recognizing all data is not easy. One thing you can do is to write down the facts. You don't have to judge the facts or label them good or bad facts, just write down the facts.

In the case of Brian, the facts would be:

1.  Barney is a 9-year-old golden lab.

2.  Barney is having seizures, is vomiting and lethargic.

3.  The vet confirmed a medical condition of a brain tumor causing these symptoms.

Other facts to then consider would include:

1.  Brian is having difficulty accepting the medical reality of his dog.

2.  Brian may be avoiding talking about Barney's physical health in the hope of avoiding the feeling. *He still feels discomfort even though he is not talking to anyone.* Avoiding the feeling doesn't make them go away.

Writing down the facts can be a helpful strategy to be able to more objectively look at a situation. Try to stick to facts versus how you feel about the facts. Facts, by definition, are data that anyone could confirm. After you look at the facts of the situation, allow yourself to explore your options moving forward. In order to accept reality, it's important to take an honest assessment of the situation.

## ANALYZING AVERY

Going back to Avery's story, a documentation of the facts could be helpful to seeing the big picture.

For Avery, the facts would be:

1.  Avery's current weight.
2.  The range she falls on a height/weight/gender/age chart, documenting the fact that she is underweight.
3.  Avery's daily caloric intake, which is severely under the recommended amount for an 18-year-old female.
4.  Symptoms Avery is experiencing such as low energy, low food intake, isolation, confusion, difficulty concentrating.
5.  She is unwilling to talk about what is going on for her.
6.  She has a good support system in her family and extended family.

Once the facts are documented (good and bad), Avery can begin to take an honest assessment of her situation and make choices on how to move forward. It helps to accept the situation, see the big picture, and assess options for moving forward.

Change the thought from: **"It's too overwhelming to talk about what is happening."** to **"I might feel uncomfortable talking about this, but maybe if I talk, I can understand other ways to cope with my feelings."**

Here are some exercises to consider if it is difficult to open up about experiences and feelings:

1. What pain is being avoided? Identify the feeling. Learning to do this might require going through a day and labeling what you might be feeling. Identifying the feeling helps clarify the reality of the situation and opens options for making choices on how to move forward.

2. Consider whether there is purpose for the pain. What might you learn from having this experience?

3. Consider that avoiding the feeling keeps you in purgatory. You don't totally avoid the feelings, but also don't move through them. Contemplate ways to identify and express difficult feelings. Perhaps you could discuss them with a safe friend, a therapist, journaling, or through art. Feeling overwhelmed can turn into feeling empowered.

4. Write down the facts of the situation (both good and bad). Documenting the facts helps to accept the situation.

# KEY SUMMARY POINTS

The main idea of this chapter focuses on the thought that someone doesn't want to go to treatment because they believe treatment will be too intense and they don't want to feel their feelings.

Drill down to discover what is really driving this thought. Options include:

1.  Learning to identify feelings.
2.  Understanding the purpose behind pain.
3.  Recognizing that working to avoid feelings doesn't actually avoid the feelings. It's hard to hold them down and eventually, they will come out.
4.  Objectively look at the facts of the situation.

The goal of working to identify, feel, and move through painful feelings can be done with a therapist, and it can be useful to have a conversation with someone who is hesitant to engage in this process about how avoidance of painful feelings doesn't actually avoid the pain.

## DECISION TREE

**Prompt:** "I don't want to consider treatment because it is too hard to open up/my feelings are too intense."

What are your thoughts about getting help?

"It's too hard to open up. My feelings are too intense."

What are your thoughts about getting help?

"I don't want to feel..."
- Consider what feeling is being avoided and if that's working.
- Consider whether there is purpose in the pain.
- Is avoiding the feeling keeping you in feeling purgatory?

"I don't want to talk about..."
- Identify the facts.
- Accept facts/reality of the situation.

# CHAPTER 6

# "I CAN HANDLE IT ON MY OWN"

THIS CHAPTER HIGHLIGHTS how to talk to someone who isn't seeking help because they want to handle it on their own. This chapter starts with Nick's story to illustrate an example of how to talk to someone who believes this thought about treatment. The chapter ends with suggestions for how to change someone's mind when they believe this thought.

## NICK'S STORY: A CASE STUDY

I live in the woods in North Carolina. Alone. I prefer not being around people. I walk the woods and have gotten to know them pretty well. I'm comfortable here. Nature makes sense. It's cruel out here, but there is purpose. Everything is just trying to survive. Humans, on the other hand, are just cruel.

I'm watching a herd of deer eat grass. Watching them calms me. Seems my heartrate and breathing slow when I'm with deer. A couple of herds move through my yard daily. The doe and fawn run in one group, with the fawn close to their moms. Two herds of bucks also come through most days. The bucks don't mingle but will tolerate each other unless I have carrots. Sometimes that will get them showing their dominant side. Each herd has a dominant buck. He's the leader. Perhaps not ironically, he's also the one with the biggest antlers. The bucks fight on occasion. You can tell that sometimes it's for play and sometimes more serious.

I sit with them most days. Like I said, being with them calms me. Occasionally I talk to them. Not much, but a little. I might say, "You're okay." Not sure why I say that. Maybe I just want things to be okay. Clearly, it's not great to be a deer. Not much protects them. Still. They calm my nerves.

One time I was sitting with them and two bucks got into it with each other. They do a low growl when mad that is funny to hear, except it's clear they are pissed. The big buck growled and went after the other, but the other was a lot smaller. Can't help but stick up for the little guy so I got in the middle to intervene.

Would be ironic to be eviscerated by a deer in my own yard. The very ones that calm me. But then I remembered the other day when I stretched my arms in the air, the deer got startled. I wondered if they thought I suddenly had big antlers, even though it was only my arms up in the air. So, when this big buck went after the smaller guy, I put my arms in the air. I'll be damned if it didn't do the trick. Big guy backed off.

Out here, I don't think about the war or what I saw. I deployed to Afghanistan in 2012 and spent a year there. My job in the Army was similar to being a photojournalist. Part of my job was to photograph and document. We worked with the villagers and built relationships with some of the leaders in the village. It was never clear who you could trust or not, but we did the best we could (meaning we basically couldn't trust any of them). Whenever something bad would happen, like an attack on an American, we would go to these folks for information on who was responsible. Sometimes the leader would redirect blame onto an innocent, even a child. I often wondered if they knew who was responsible and tried to redirect us so we wouldn't know the truth, or if they just wanted to appear cooperative. But usually they would lie. Their world is harsh. Several times I took pictures of beatings of children. One time an IED exploded, and my captain went to the villagers who pointed at a child being responsible. The child was whipped and beaten in the town square in front of my captain to demonstrate that they took this situation seriously. They beat an innocent child. Photographing the beating of this child haunts me. The expressions of horror and pain on the boy. He was probably only around 11 years old. No one stepped in to rescue him. No one stopped the beating. No one wanted the "blame" redirected at them. Sitting there shooting photos was unbearable. As a photographer, I zoom in on the details. I could see every horrific blow. I have a lot of pictures like this from my time over there. I saw what people are capable of.

It left me broken.

I became vocal about my objections to these beatings, but my captain was a shithead and I think he kinda liked the brutality. He got in my face that whoever was responsible needed to be punished. Maybe he wasn't a bad guy, my captain, but he didn't see anyone as innocent or that any of this was wrong. Maybe he also was broken.

In the end, I had a collection of photos from my time in the country.

The worst was when we found one of the women who had been working with us shot dead on the street. She was an older woman, maybe 50. No nonsense, smart. She didn't speak English but our translator told us what she said. She didn't like us, didn't like anything about the war. She laid out the truth as she saw it. We went to her frequently and I got to appreciate her direct, no bs, style of communication. Finding her shot dead and laid out in the street by herself was a bad day. A country that has no respect for women and children was more than I could take. I wasn't sure if we were helping or causing more harm just by being there.

I was trying not to think about my time in Afghanistan one day when I found one of the bucks shot dead in the woods. This particular buck was kinda a loner. He followed the herd, but always stayed a step behind. When the herd would come through, I would hold a couple carrots back for him to take when the rest would move on. He had a habit of holding his tongue out to the side. Kinda goofy. I have a bunch of photos of him after eating carrots, holding his tongue out like that. Not sure why someone killed him. It's pretty clear that his death was slow and painful. I can trace back the blood trail to see how far he had gone. Thought I lost the trail a couple of times but found it again.

People suck.

A couple days have gone by since I found the dead buck and they have been hard ones. I can't shake the images in my head. In my mind, I keep seeing the dead buck and then I see the dead woman from Afghanistan. I have nightmares where I wake up screaming because someone is about to be shot and I want to warn them, but I'm never in time. Every time I go outside, I think that I might find something else dead. I can't live like this. I don't even want to walk in the woods because I'm afraid of what I might find. What damage some asshole has done. I don't trust anymore. I can't go in grocery stores because there are children in there with their moms, and it reminds me of the children in Afghanistan who were whipped. Innocent children. I can't be in a grocery store and hear a kid's voice without needing to walk right out of there. I avoid looking at my pictures from Afghanistan because I don't think I can take it. Hard enough that the images live in my brain like they do. I don't need the actual images. I put cameras around my yard to make sure no one is in my territory and check the cameras about 50 times a day. I can't pick up the phone when it rings or respond to texts. I don't want to engage with anyone. I don't want to hear what anyone has to say. If they hear that I'm struggling, they will tell me I should get help. I should go to the VA and get treatment. I'm not going to get treatment though. I'm not the one that has the problem. I'm not the one going around beating up innocent children and killing innocent women and animals. Plus, I can handle this by myself. As long as I don't see or talk to anyone.

It's been a bit since I found the dead buck and I'm still struggling. I decide to take a walk in the woods and on the way back along the road by my house and I pass another dead animal on the side of the road. Looks like he might have been hit by a car. He's got blood on his head. A possum. Another asshole human driving too fast probably. As I'm walking, a car pulls along the side of the road and a woman gets out. She pulls a box out of her backseat and walks over to the dead possum. When she crouches next to it, the possum stands up and walks around in a circle. What the hell. I guess it's not dead.

"What are you going to do with it?" I ask her.

"Assess. Probably give it some fluids and medicine. Someone called me and let me know there was an injured animal," she responds.

"You think it'll live?"

"Not sure. Good sign it's moving. Bad sign it's turning in circles. Sign of a head injury."

"What will you do with it if it lives?"

"Rehab and release it back to its home."

"So it can just get hit again by some other asshole?"

She doesn't respond. Starts talking instead to the possum. "Poor baby. It's okay. Let's get a look at you and see how you're doing. Poor little guy."

"Is it a guy?" I'm just standing there watching her and can't seem to walk on just yet.

"Not sure if it's male or female. I'll check when I get it home."

"You do this in your home? Bring home an injured possum?"

"I do."

"How many possum do you have in your home?"

She laughs at this question and says, "Well, we have a lot of animals. We have five dogs, nine cats, 42 kittens who need homes, 28 squirrels, ten raccoons, and three possums. Well, maybe four possums now."

"In your home?"

"Yep." She lifts the possum that she has wrapped in a towel and keeps talking to it. I half-expect the critter to hiss and bite at her, but it seems to like her just fine.

"How many of the animals will you release?"

"I hope we find homes for all of the kittens, and we try and release all of the wildlife if we are able. There are two raccoons and one squirrel that can't live in the wild, so they stay with us."

"How many die?"

She looks at me with an intensity that feels familiar and says, "Some of them die."

Wish I had my camera on me. This is a scene I'd like to document, just like I documented scenes in Afghanistan. Not all the scenes in Afghanistan were bad. Some were. But some were not. Sometimes you find an image of something pure and beautiful, like the mountainside or a tree. Sometimes you even find beauty in a human, just not very often. This woman seems to like taking care of hurt animals and she must lose a bunch of them given the look she just gave me.

"Why? Why do you do it?"

She looks at me again with that intense stare and doesn't say anything for a moment. Then she says, "Because if it were me, it's what I would want someone to do for me. You prefer I just let him die here by the side of the road?"

This time, it's me that doesn't respond. I guess I *was* thinking that critters die by themselves.

She goes on to say, "I'm not sure I can explain why I help animals. I guess it's cause I can. My place is to care for the injured. I don't question it; I just do it. Maybe the world is like one big ant hill. Or beehive. You know how when there is damage to the hill or the hive, all the workers kick in and start to repair it? It's beautiful they do that. Coordinated efforts to make things right again. Doesn't matter if there are hundreds of ants working towards reparation or just one. What matters is that something is out there fixing the mess. And I guess my job is this. In a world where sometimes things don't make sense, this makes sense to me. This is my job. My way of helping."

Again, I'm quiet. I like the concept that people have jobs and do their jobs, but it's hard to understand how some people believe their job is destruction and death. That part doesn't make sense.

That's when she asks me what my job is. What do I do? "I'm a journalist. A photographer. Wish I had my camera today actually."

"Yeah? What would you photograph?"

"A good person in this crazy world."

I've been sitting back since Afghanistan. Not sure what else to do. Not sure why I'm standing here talking to this woman. I don't talk to many people anymore. And I sure don't share much about myself, but it seems I have nothing to lose. "I work a little for the local newspaper, but I haven't been doing much since I returned from Afghanistan. People in my family say I need help. That I should go to the VA and talk to someone, but I think I can handle my own business."

"Well, maybe you can. Maybe you can't. But if you're anything like this possum, you're going to have an easier time healing if you get assessed and treated. Not sure what you're dealing with, but what are you doing to heal?"

"Guess I hoped time would help. And not being around people."

"Is it helping?"

My thoughts flash to waking up because of nightmares and how much I want to avoid people and the crap they do. Can't say what I'm doing is helping exactly. Maybe I could talk to someone. My way isn't making anything worse, but it's not making anything better either. It would be nice to be able to sleep again and not have nightmares. "Thought it was. Maybe it's not though. Maybe it was just a time out."

"If I give this possum a moment out here alone, a time out, he's going to die. It's possible with a little treatment and rehab he can go back to a healthy life living on his own."

"Are you saying I'm like the possum?"

"I don't know if you're like the possum or not, but it sounds like you're saying you've been suffering. Maybe it would help to talk to someone with more experience in treating what hurt you. At a minimum, it sounds like your treatment plan is not working as well as you'd like it to. What do you have to lose by talking to someone?"

"I'd be annoyed."

"So. Be annoyed. This possum may not be too happy with me today either, but I bet by tomorrow he and I will be friends. And he'll at least have some food and medicine and shelter. If you don't like your doctor, you can always stop going. But you won't know if you don't try."

She has a point. Maybe I have nothing to lose. This possum will die without her. Am I like the possum? I signed up to serve in the military to do good. To serve. I believed in the mission. Now I'm not sure that we did any good at all, but maybe I still have options. Maybe I can serve in a different way. "How do you become someone that helps animals?" I ask her.

"There are courses you can take. Would you like information on them?"

"Actually, yes. You've given me a lot to think about. I would like to learn about the courses."

"I'll send it to you."

Maybe I can still do good. Might be worth looking into the VA for treatment. Maybe they'll teach me how to sleep without nightmares. Then I can look into courses and help wildlife. That might feel good.

# AN ANALYSIS OF NICK'S STORY

Nick is experiencing several symptoms associated with post-traumatic stress disorder (PTSD).

PTSD is characterized by four symptoms, including:

1. **Avoidance.** Avoidance symptoms include things like avoiding people, places and things associated with a traumatic event and isolating.
2. **Hypervigilance.** Hypervigilance includes being on alert, angry, or irritable.
3. **Re-experiencing.** Re-experiencing is when someone has vivid memories of a traumatic event (i.e., flashbacks or nightmares).
4. **Negative thoughts and feelings.**

Nick is experiencing several PTSD symptoms. He isolates and spends time alone in the woods; is vigilant with cameras and on alert for injured animals; has flashbacks and nightmares of his time in a warzone (seeing the woman shot and the child beat in Afghanistan); and has negative thoughts and feelings about man.

Nick believes that he needs time alone and doesn't need help because he can handle it on his own. In the story, we see that Nick modified his thoughts about seeking help during a discussion with a wildlife rehabber. The wildlife rehabber pointed out that injured animals die without help, but with a little medical attention they are able to release many injured animals back to their environment. This discussion helped Nick to see that he might benefit from speaking with an expert on PTSD and, importantly, that he still may have purpose in the world. He signed up for the military initially because he wanted to be helpful to his country and community. He realized that he could still be helpful to his community and decided to also sign up for a wildlife rehab course.

His initial thoughts on getting help were:

| INITIAL THOUGHTS |
| --- |
| "I can handle this on my own." |
| "Hard to turn to others for help. Don't trust people." |
| **INITIAL FEELINGS** |
| Hopeless |
| Agitated |
| Loss of faith in mankind |
| **INITIAL BEHAVIORS** |
| Isolate |
| Avoidance of people, places and things associated with trauma |
| His thoughts changed during the discussion on the side of the street with Wildlife Rehabber. |
| **NEW THOUGHTS** |
| "I can handle this on my own but I'm not doing well." |
| "It's hard to turn to others for help, but there might be some good people out there." |
| "Maybe I can find a different way to serve and do good." |
| **NEW FEELINGS** |
| Slightly hopeful |
| **NEW BEHAVIORS** |
| Research vet centers and places to seek assistance for PTSD |
| Take classes on caring for injured wildlife. |

# WORKING THROUGH RESISTANCE TO TREATMENT

Many people who don't want to get help for mental health or substance use disorders prefer to handle things on their own. They might not trust the healthcare system or they just believe that they can address the situation and deal with it on their own. The truth is that some people *do* handle things on their own and do fairly well. It's important, critical even, to assess whether an individual is truly "handling" things or whether they are avoiding. People can work through mental health and substance use issues if they are being addressed (with or without professional involvement); but it is important that things are being addressed.

The next section of this chapter will focus on how to have conversations with individuals who would prefer to handle any mental health or substance use issues on their own; and ways you can help someone reconsider these thoughts to make a decision about getting help.

Someone wanting to handle things on their own might say things like:

- I can handle it by myself.
- I don't trust others enough to talk to them about my life.
- I can control things on my own.

If someone in your life is refusing treatment and saying these thoughts, there are a variety of ways to have a discussion with them to get them to reconsider these thoughts.

These include discussions about:

1. Formalize the self-treatment plan. Define your goals/ strategies.

2. Recognize the fight as yours and yours alone (or theirs and theirs alone if you are trying to help someone).

3. Engage in social support and coping skills.

# FORMALIZING A SELF-TREATMENT PLAN

## WRITE IT DOWN

The first step is to document the "treatment" plan and write it all down, same as if you were seeing a professional. Doctors and therapists use tested, evidence-based protocols and treatments. They use data to know which treatments work for specific symptoms. The provider explains the treatment protocol they are following. For example, a physician might prescribe an antidepressant to treat depression. They can give data on when the medication will begin to work and what to expect in terms of efficacy and side effects. Same is true for psychotherapy. A therapist can specify the protocol they are following, what to expect and when it will begin to work. A self-treatment plan should follow that same format.

When following a self-treatment plan, formalize it. Write it down. Write down the specific treatment **goal**. Then, specify the **strategies** that will be used to work towards that goal. It is important to be specific on both goals and treatment strategies. Try to make the goals and strategies as objective as possible.

Goals/strategies should be:

1. **Specific** ("Walk for 10 minutes per day" vs. "Get more exercise")
2. **Measurable** (quantify the goal using measurement)
3. **Achievable** (something that can be accomplished)
4. **Relevant** (to the individual and the goal)
5. **Time limited** (immediate, short-term goals)
6. **Sustainable** (something that the individual can continue to do)

For example, "Be happier" is hard to quantify. You might know it when you feel it, but it's hard to measure. Better to have a quantifiable goal such as, "Spend at least two hours per day engaged in pleasurable activities, such as..."

To identify a goal that would be considered specific, relevant, time-limited, achievable, sustainable, and measurable, let's say an individual wants to be happier and less isolated. A goal and related strategies to achieve this goal might look something like:

**Goal:** Be happier and less isolated. Reduce depressive thoughts. Increase the amount of time per day focused on pleasure.

**Strategies**

- Spend 10 minutes each morning for one month identifying ten things that I am good at. Write these down.
- Spend 10 minutes each morning for one month identifying ten things that I am grateful for. Write these down.

- Identify three people to talk to each week for at least 30 minutes each.

- Engage in an activity that is pleasurable for at least 1 hour per day.

The more specific the goal and the strategies are to achieve that goal, the more likely the goal will be achieved. It will also be easier to identify which parts of the strategy work and which parts do not.

## OPTIMIZATION

Some self-treatment plans optimize opportunities for success and others maintain the status quo. In other words, there are strategies that might work and strategies that might not work as well to achieve the desired goal.

An example of a strategy that may not work to achieve the goal, for example, is in the story of Nick. Nick intended to manage his symptoms of PTSD on his own.

His self-treatment plan included:

1. Avoid people/places/things that remind him of trauma in Afghanistan.
2. Spend time in the woods.
3. Isolate and avoid contact with humans.

Notice that his goal was to reduce his distress from his time in Afghanistan. He found comfort spending time in the woods and interacting with animals. His strategies, however, did not decrease nightmares or help him avoid distressing memories. In order to achieve his goal, it might be worthwhile to consult with an expert on PTSD for additional evidence-based strategies.

Another example of a strategy that may not work or optimize a desired goal is "Joseph." Joseph wants to self-treat his addiction to alcohol.

His self-treatment plan includes:

1.  Drink when the urge comes to drink.

2.  Avoid anyone who doesn't approve of his drinking.

3.  Try not to think about the consequences of his drinking.

Notice that his goal is to reduce drinking, but his strategies don't give an opportunity for him to achieve his goal.

We see this type of self-treatment plan often with disorders of addiction and anxiety. In terms of anxiety, someone with anxiety might prefer to self-treat their sensitivity to anxiety by avoiding anything that makes them anxious. Their treatment goal is to avoid anxiety. For example, let's say someone doesn't like social situations. They feel better (less anxious) at home. Being in public is anxiety provoking for them, so their treatment plan is to avoid social situations. They feel less anxious and "successful" at home. The problem is that their condition isn't being treated but instead reinforced. This individual will continue to avoid situations that increase their anxiety instead of learning to move through or manage anxious feelings. **The goal is to reduce anxiety, but the strategies end up increasing anxiety long-term.**

# STRATEGIES THAT MAY OPTIMIZE OR IMPROVE SYMPTOMS

On the other hand, let's consider self-treatment plans that might work to improve symptoms. Natalie (like Joseph in the example above) has an addiction to alcohol.

Her self-treatment plan includes:

1. Reduce drinking from seven days a week to two days a week.
2. Enforce a boundary on the number of drinks per day (maximum of three drinks per day).
3. Specify individuals that will help her enforce her quantity/frequency goals (friends Tashia and Aida).
4. Look for opportunities to engage in activities to replace drinking (examples may include taking the dog for a walk, cleaning the house, exercising, getting a massage, hiking, reading a book, calling a friend, etc.).

Natalie's self-treatment plan uses strategies for her to reduce her alcohol intake and achieve her goal. She creates opportunities to discover which aspects of her self-treatment plan are easy to implement and which are hard. She may want to consult with other individuals who have had success reducing their alcohol use to learn tricks that worked for them. Some people have been successful with the "cold turkey" approach to reducing substance use. Others have found these approaches difficult and prefer to slowly reduce their use. Either way, learning what works best for a specific individual is important.

**Be honest about which strategies work best to achieve goals.** In order to be successful, there must be honesty. Strategies that maintain symptoms do not work.

## SELF-TREATMENT PLAN

When self-treating, remember to:

1.  Define/formalize treatment goal(s). Be specific.

2.  Define the strategies to achieve the goal. Make sure strategies are specific, relevant, time-limited, sustainable, achievable, and measurable.

3.  Honestly assess your plans strengths and weaknesses to achieve your goal(s).

4.  Check in on a weekly basis to track progress on achieving goal(s).

5.  Have a back-up plan.

6.  Define when you will implement the back-up plan.

7.  Consider what markers need to be present for seeking professional help. This is the, "When all else fails, I'll call for help" option.

Let's take a look at a couple of examples of self-treatment plans in action:

# CARRIE'S GOAL: WEIGHT LOSS

Carrie is a 45-year-old female who is overweight and wants to lose weight. She does not want to seek professional help and wants to achieve weight loss on her own. Her self-treatment plan is:

**Formalize Self-Treatment Strategies (BE SPECIFIC):**

- Eat vegetables at least twice per day
- Eliminate fast food
- Reduce the number of sodas to one per day

**Treatment Goal (BE SPECIFIC):**

- Lose 30 pounds in 6 months

**Strengths/Weaknesses of Plan:**

- **Strength:** Eliminating certain foods (fast food/soda) will benefit weight loss and overall health.
- **Strength:** Eating more vegetables may increase the nutritional value of the foods she is eating.
- **Weakness:** No tracking of the number of calories eaten per day
- **Weakness:** Assessment of nutritional content is missing
- **Weakness:** Exercise is missing

**Weekly Progress:**

- She will track weight and hopes to lose 1 to 2 pounds per week for 24 weeks.

**Back-up Plans:**

- Consult with a weight loss expert
- Use a calorie tracker

**Define When to Implement Back-up Plan:**

- She will give it 3–4 weeks to see if her initial plan is working to lose 1–2 pounds per week. By week 4, she would need to see weight loss of 4–8 pounds to stay on her original self-treatment plan.

**Consider Professional Help:**

- She will consider seeking professional help if her self-treatment plan does not achieve her goal.

## NICK'S GOAL: PTSD MANAGEMENT

Nick is a 35-year-old male who is struggling with symptoms of PTSD. His self-treatment plan is:

**Formalize Self-Treatment Strategies (BE SPECIFIC):**

- Avoid people/places/things that remind him of traumatic events.

- Spend time with animals in the woods.

- Isolate and reduce interactions with humans.

**Treatment Goal (BE SPECIFIC):**

- Reduce distress. Be able to sleep and breathe in peace.

**Strengths/Weaknesses of Plan:**

- **Strength:** Give himself time to help his mind/body to recover.

- **Strength:** Engage in pleasurable activities (time in woods, time with animals).

- **Weakness:** Not directly addressing memories and feelings associated with the trauma allows for repeated triggers.

- **Weakness:** Still having thoughts and memories even though avoiding people, places, things associated with the trauma.

- **Weakness:** Still having nightmares.

**Weekly Progress:**

- No specific plan in place to assess for progress.

**Back-up Plans:**

- No back-up plan.

**Define When to Implement Back-up Plan:**

- Not considered.

**Consider Professional Help:**

- Nick wants to handle his situation on his own and is having difficulty with his faith in man. Because he is struggling with trust, it is hard for him to seek help. For Nick to work through this belief, he might need to remember interactions with humans that were pleasant and encouraging. For example, it might be true that Nick has seen humans who engage in dark and cruel behavior, but he has probably also seen humans who engage in beautiful and helpful behavior.

Overall, self-treatment plans are more likely to be successful if they are defined and if the individual follows through on the strategies to achieve the goal.

## REALITY CHECK: YOU *ARE* ON YOUR OWN

A second strategy to consider when working with someone who wants to handle their situation on their own is to have an honest conversation about what it means to "handle it on their own."

The reality is that *we are on our own.* Yes, people are influential; but there is no magic wand. Life will still have pain. You have the choice of whether or not to deal with it and the choice on how to deal with it. A therapist can help you better understand why you engage in certain behaviors or help you identify your thoughts on certain situations, but it's still YOU that has to implement change.

It might be important to understand what "handle it on their own" means to that individual. Some people value self-sufficiency, while others have enormous difficulty asking for help.

- What does "ask for help" mean to that individual?

- Does it remind them of someone in their life that they didn't like or respect?

- Did they learn somewhere along the way that others will not help them, so they have to do it all on their own anyway? If yes, how does this impact them?

- Are there opportunities when it is okay to ask for help? Would it be okay to ask for help on a physical problem, a financial problem, an emotional problem, a logistical problem, a family problem?

- Are there a few individuals who it is okay to ask for help or do they truly shy away from asking anyone for any- thing ever?

Teasing out the meaning behind the thought "handle it on my own" is important. Remember, we *are* all on our own:

1.  There is no magic wand to take pain away.

2.  Unfortunately, we are quite skilled at lying to ourselves about magic pills and being on our own. Therapists are trained to see how people talk to themselves and can be helpful at identifying unconscious ways people stay stuck.

Let's look at some examples of the potential lies people tell themselves.

**Example 1:** "I'll feel better after a beer."

-   There is no magical ingredient in beer that takes away a stressful life. You can tell yourself that beer has magical powers and choose to believe that while drinking a beer, you feel better, momentarily, but it actually does nothing to SOLVE a problem. **The magic is in the words you tell yourself about beer.** And if the magic is in the words that you tell yourself, you can change the words and turn the magic elsewhere.

-   Excessive drinking of beer can lead to side effects that don't feel better at all (headache, confusion, nausea, poor decisions, brain cell death)

-   Whatever situation that caused that bad feeling will still be there during and after drinking the beer.

-   Consider changing the thought, "I'll feel better after a beer" to, "I don't want to deal with this situation right now but will address it tomorrow. There are a variety of things that could make me feel better in the meantime."

**Example 2:** Grown adult tantrums when they want something. Parent of that adult tells themselves, "I'll give them what they want. They are my child and I love them. I'm a good parent."

- Adults (whether they are your child or not) are responsible for meeting their own needs.

- Meeting their needs for them does not teach self-sufficiency. It does not help them be self-sufficient and rely on themselves.

- Meeting their needs for them creates dependence/ resentment/enmeshment.

- Giving them what they "want" because of a tantrum actually increases tantrums. If someone said, I'll give you a dollar every time you tantrum, I'd tantrum all day. Consider what is being reinforced.

- Boundaries are *essential* in all relationships.

Notice in both examples that an individual has a thought (i.e., "I'll feel better after a beer" or "I'll just give them what they want") in order to manage stress. The resulting behavior comes directly from these thoughts. If you say to yourself, I'll feel better after a beer, you are likely to have a beer. If you say to yourself, I'll give them what they want, you are likely to give them whatever they want. In both cases, the behaviors may be fine or they may be problematic. It's important to consider how your own thoughts influence what you do in any particular situation. If your thoughts control your behavior, then it's great to know that it's as easy as changing your thoughts to change your behavior.

# SOCIAL SUPPORT AND COPING SKILLS

## SOCIAL SUPPORT

Social disconnection is a transdiagnostic factor that contributes to bad outcomes. If you hold all other factors constant, individuals that are lonely and disconnected from others have worse outcomes for *all* disease states. Whether we like it or not, we are social beings. Belonging is a basic human need, along with food/water, air, and safety. Social connection matters. While social relationships matter, it is okay to take a time-out to recharge. It is also okay to put up boundaries with toxic individuals in your life. But wherever you find good humans, spend some time with them. If you are having a hard time finding good humans, consider working with a therapist. They can help connect you. Finding social support in life, even during the good times, is a human *need*. **Finding social support during difficult times is a critical need.**

## COPING SKILLS

Chapter 7 discusses coping skills in more detail. The bottom line is that everyone should be able to identify a long list of coping skills to get through life. It is difficult to only rely on one or two, we need many of them and especially during difficult times.

# KEY SUMMARY POINTS

The main idea of this chapter is to focus on someone who wants to handle the situation on their own.

Strategies to help guide discussions about treatment with an individual who wants to handle the situation on their own include:

1.  Formalize the self-treatment plan.
2.  Recognize the fight as yours and yours alone.
3.  Engage in social support and coping skills.

## DECISION TREE

**Prompt:** "I don't want to consider treatment because I can handle it on my own."

What are your thoughts about getting help?

"I can handle it on my own. I don't *need* help."

Document treatment by:
1. Identifying your goal
2. Identifying strategies to achieve that goal
3. Have a plan B and reassess to see if the plan is working

Recognize you are on your own (whether you seek help or not).

Identify coping skills and available support systems.

# CHAPTER 7

# "I'M NOT READY"

**T**HIS CHAPTER HIGHLIGHTS how to talk to someone who isn't seeking help because they believe they are not ready for treatment. The chapter starts with David's story to illustrate an example of how to talk to someone who believes this thought. The chapter ends with suggestions for how to change someone's mind who believes this thought.

## DAVID'S STORY: A CASE STUDY

Standing in the kitchen, where he made a mess, he can see his bedroom door, closed. He knows she is inside, probably sitting on the bed, angry, and breathing with flared nostrils in that way she has that makes her face ugly. She's waiting for him. Waiting for him to make things good again, like he always does. He can talk his way out of anything. No matter what he's done, he can convince people that it's all good.

It's not working as well as it used to, though. Used to be that he'd lose his temper, apologize the next day, and celebrate making things right with a beer. Or ten. Now, his "celebrations" do little to ease his mind. It's not just his mind that's unsettled, but his stomach doesn't feel good either. Feels like ants are running around in there. He used to be able to tune out anything bothering him but now his mind isn't calm. He can't focus on one thought at a time long enough to think anything through. Thoughts buzz in his brain that make no sense and irritate him.

He knows he went too far last night, but it's hard to remember the details. He was watching Sports Center on ESPN, listening to has-been football players talk about games played over the weekend. He was looking forward to dinner. It was spaghetti night, and he loves spaghetti night. Sopping up the pasta sauce with garlic bread hits all the senses. He can smell the garlic and taste the melted butter along with the acidity of the tomatoes from the sauce. He loves it when it's warm and has just a little bite of crunch from the crust of the bread. He even likes how it sounds, all slurpy and messy. That's what he was thinking about. Football, garlic bread, and beer. Okay, well, maybe he'd already had about eight or twelve beers by that point. Still, everything was chill and he was ready to eat. That's when he heard his girlfriend talking to his 12-year-old son in the kitchen and he heard his son say, "I'm never going to drink when I get older."

As soon as he heard his son say the words, he felt heat run through his body and wanted to punch the kid right through the throat. You'd think he'd be happy to hear his son declare his forever abstinence from alcohol. It's not like he didn't think the same thing when he was a kid watching his own father struggle with drinking. He knows what an alcoholic looks like, and it was his dad. Not him! His son is lucky. At least he's not at bars every damn night, coming home picking fights with everyone. That's what a real alcoholic looks like. At least he has a job, unlike his own dad who couldn't keep a job because he got in fights all the time.

So, his son insinuating he's an alcoholic like his dad pissed him off. Made him hate the kid. What does he think he's got it all figured out at the ripe age of 12? Looking back, he could've just yelled into the kitchen, "Good for you," ate his dinner, and called it a night. But that's not what happened.

Everything gets on his nerves lately and people are constantly pissing him off. Why didn't his son just shut his mouth? Both of his sons have been making comments about his drinking lately. And last night he couldn't let it go. It felt like rocket fuel erupted inside his brain and he needed to explode on the kid. He remembers screaming things like, "What are you too good for that?" and "You think your shit don't stink?" He remembers seeing his sons' eyes get big and fear on his face and feeling even more rage rip right through him. Kid is lucky he didn't rip his face off. Things got a little confusing and fuzzy after that, but he knows one of the kitchen table chairs was broken and he remembers his girlfriend in his face screaming and his kid crying, but he can't quite put all the pieces together. He's sure they all think it's his fault but it's not. They just need to leave things alone sometimes.

Now it's morning. They didn't leave him alone. They caused problems and now he has to be the one to make things right. He walks into his bedroom and sees his girlfriend folding her clothes. As soon as he walks in the room, she hits him with, "Get help."

Get help? What is she talking about? Why would he get help? She's been nagging on him for his drinking lately but stopping drinking will make everything worse. And then he'll want to drink even more, so what's the point? Besides, he likes drinking. It tastes good and it calms him down. It used to calm him down. Sometimes it calms him down. Okay, nothing calms him anymore, but alcohol is the one thing that used to work. He can't imagine how he would deal with life if he didn't have alcohol.

He intended to walk into his bedroom that morning, smooth things over with the girlfriend, and for everything to be okay. But she said, "Get help," grabbed her clothes, and left. Which meant, the only person left to talk to was his son. And he had to admit, he wasn't confident he could make things right with his son. He remembers back when he was a kid, and his dad would try and make things right after coming home drunk and getting violent. Didn't matter what the old man would say the next day because there was nothing he could say to make it right. The only thing he wanted was his dad to stop drinking.

Screw this. He doesn't need this bullshit. He can't remember if he ate last night, but he's pretty sure he finished that bottle of whiskey to deal with the stress his kid caused. He needs food.

He gets in his car and heads to the diner on Main Street. He figures he can eat a burger and think through his next move once he has food in his system and his head stops pounding. He pulls into a parking spot across the street from the diner and starts to feel more optimistic. Things will fall back in place; he knows they will. They always have. He smells bacon and onions as he walks through the door. There are plenty of open seats at the counter and his favorite waitress, Diane, is working. She catches his eye as he comes through the door, "Hiya. Be right with you in a sec." See? Things are already falling back into place.

He sits at the counter by himself and settles into watching one of the TV's. That TV has golf on, which is just as well. He can't concentrate on watching anything anyway.

"Hi David. What would you like to order?" Diane asks.

"Burger and coke," he says. She nods and walks away. Just like he likes it. No bullshit, no drama. This is the kind of place where you can sit for a second and gather your thoughts. She brings a coke to him and places it on the counter. He'd like to drink it but isn't sure how it will sit in his stomach. He feels a little queasy. He better wait for food before he takes a drink. As he waits for his burger, he glances to his right and notices an old man and woman he's never seen before sitting a couple chairs over. Diane walks over to them and asks what they would like to order. "Liver and onions," the man says.

"We need a Sid Special!" Diane yells into the kitchen. The cook comes out with a big smile and says, "We'll have that right out for you, Sid."

Whatever. The cook is a fat old fart. I guess that comes with being around food all day. Man, his head is pounding. He's ready to eat some food.

Meanwhile, the old man and woman are looking at each other and smiling. They must be 90 years old. The woman orders a coke and chicken salad and says to the man, "I'm glad I'm not the one cooking liver for you. Smells up the house for days." They both laugh, and Diane asks them how they've been.

"Still above ground," the man says with a smirk. "Sid had another run in with turkeys this morning," the woman says.

Diane says, "Uh oh. What happened this time?"

Sid says, "Goddamn turkeys messing with my plants. She loves blueberries, you know," and points at his wife.

The woman says, "And he loves my blueberry pie."

"Damn right I do! I planted blueberry bushes and put down mulch straw and damn turkeys come out this morning and kicked my straw all over the place!"

The woman says, "I had to yell at him to put his clothes on when he goes running outside shooing 'em away. He runs out muttering about turkeys, flailing his arms, yelling, 'Gobble, gobble. Gobble.' Meanwhile, the turkeys are running around with their wings out trying to get away from him also screeching, 'Gobble, gobble, gobble.'"

As Diane laughs, the cook yells out of the kitchen, "You tell those turkeys, Sid! I bet they were running to get away from your naked ass!"

As they all laugh, Sid says, "I just want them to leave her blueberries alone. She'll make blueberry pie come August." And again, the man and woman look at each other smiling. The woman asks Diane about her kids and the cook asks Sid about his latest woodworking project.

David wonders to himself, (1) will they ever shut up, and (2) how do you get to be old and still smiling at each other like that? They act like they like each other. He can't imagine family liking each other. Even Diane and the cook seem to like them.

When his burger arrives, he takes a bite despite his pounding headache and gurgling stomach and someone behind him screams out, "HAPPY ANNIVERSARY!" The pounding in his head is now so great that he's worried he's going to hurl right there at the counter of the diner. He turns to glare at the screaming asshole and sees them hugging the old lady. The old man is smiling and patting the asshole on the back. What the fuck. He comes to the diner to eat and get some peace and quiet and ends up smack dab at a festival of loud, old people. He hears them talking about how the old couple has been married for 60 years.

He manages to eat a couple bites of the burger before he has to run to the bathroom. He barely makes it to the can before his bowels explode. Ugh. He feels like shit and now he smells like shit. Well, he probably smelled like shit before but now it's worse. And even worse than that, while he's in the bathroom, the old man walks in. Funny though, while he wants to hate the old man, he can't help but wonder how this fella managed to get people to smile at him like that. David himself seems to be surrounded by unhappy people. Feels like he's always apologizing and trying to smooth things over. And more and more, those times seem to have something to do with beer.

Thankfully Sid doesn't say anything when he walks in. Gotta give the old man credit. Most people would've walked into the bathroom and turned right around. Just the smell alone was enough to make David want to leave (and heave). If David had been the one to walk in on that same scene, he would've muttered some expletive and gotten the hell out of there. But Sid doesn't say a word. Surprisingly, it's David who initiates contact.

He asks Sid, "How do you stay married for 60 years?"

Sid replies, "Damn if I know...but I do know that when shit hits the fan, you go to the shitter, and then get off the pot."

"Yeah. I guess. But how do you stop shit from hitting the fan?" he asks.

"Hard to know, but when all else fails, just make sure they are happy."

David isn't sure he understands this. He asks, "Make sure *they* are happy?"

And with that, Sid walks out leaving David wondering what he meant.

After the shit show (literally) at the diner, he drives home feeling uneasy. It's time to talk with his son, but that old couple is still on his mind. They liked each other. Family, from his perspective, don't act like that.

Standing in the hallway outside of his sons' bedroom, he realizes:

1.   He doesn't want to be like his dad.

2.   His dad never got help. And he needed it.

3.   He doesn't have a relationship with his dad because of his dad's drinking.

4.   Drinking isn't really working out so well.

He pushes his son's bedroom door open and stops. He's standing there looking at his son, but it's like he's in his own childhood bedroom, from when he was a kid. He remembers hating his dad. Hating everything about him. God, he remembers hating the smell of his dad. He smelled like booze and cigarettes, the smell lingering even after his dad walked away. He hated his dads' eyes, guilty looking. Ashamed. Whatever his dad said was useless. He remembers his dad said the world was against him, and he was just trying his best and no one seemed to care.

Which is similar to what he was about to say to his own son. In this room. Twenty-five years later.

He backs out of the room without saying a word and goes into the kitchen. He wants a second to gather his thoughts. He needs to start doing things differently but the idea of being without alcohol terrifies him. Alcohol helps him breathe. It's the one thing he looks forward to everyday. For years now, he's told himself alcohol makes everything better.

But it's not making everything better. It's making everything worse. Still, feels like he's losing a friend.

He sits at the kitchen table looking at the broken chair lying on the floor. His son walks in the room.

"Dad?"

"Kid. I got some thinking to do."

"Why did you get so mad when I said I'm not going to drink when I'm older? Do you want me to drink?"

"No. No, I don't. I remember when I was your age, watching grandpa drink. I didn't want to be anything like him."

"Can't you just stop drinking?" he asks.

David pauses before saying, "I don't know how."

"Can someone help you?"

The old man in the diner told him that when all else fails, make *them* happy. How in the world is he supposed to do that? He doesn't know where to start. He's spent so much time justifying his reasons to continue to drink that he hadn't really considered all the reasons to stop. He doesn't know much about getting help. He knows about AA. He knows some people go to rehab for months. He doesn't like either of those options. Maybe he should call his doc. Maybe his doc will give him a medicine that could make this all right. Or maybe his doc will know someone he can talk to. It's worth a shot because physically he feels like crap. Old man said to make *them* happy. Weird, because he realizes that what would make them happy is if he got help and stopped drinking. Could everything get better if he stopped drinking? That was what he wanted for his own dad. He knows one thing for sure: he's too young to feel this old.

"It's like losing a best friend," he tells his son.

"Maybe you can find a new friend. I'll be your friend," his son tells him.

David realizes he's been putting alcohol first. He hasn't been taking care of his family or his relationship or even his own health. He's been focused on drinking. He tells his son, "I'll take you up on that. I'd like to be your friend."

## AN ANALYSIS OF DAVID'S STORY

"I like to drink." "I don't *want* to quit."

There are many people like David who don't consider getting help for their alcohol use because it's hard for them to imagine life without alcohol. And while it might be true, drinking can be enjoyable; this is rarely what someone is saying when they state they like drinking and don't want to quit. Drinking might be a way to cope with life stress or discomfort. However, enjoying an occasional drink versus relying on alcohol to manage life stresses are two different things. Therefore, it's important to acknowledge the pros and cons of drinking. Drinking might be enjoyable, (to celebrate or for taste); and drinking might be problematic (hangover or DUI). It's unwise to focus only on the benefits and ignore or minimize the consequences of alcohol use.

The next section of this chapter will focus on uncovering the meaning of statements like: "I like to drink and don't want to quit." Uncovering the meaning that drives this sentence is an important step to getting help. To believe "I like drinking and don't want to quit" means the individual will continue to drink.

And just because that thought, "I like to drink," might be true, it is also potentially **not true**. For example, David likes to drink but on deeper inspection, he realizes that drinking isn't benefiting him the way it used to. Depending on the individual, any one of the following might be motivating or driving the thought that they like drinking and don't want to quit. It may not be the case that all four of these motivations listed below are driving the thought, but any one of them might be. Uncovering the deeper meaning underlying the thought is critical to moving someone further into considering treatment.

Potential reasons why someone might state they like alcohol and don't want to quit include:

- **Coping skills (Coping with alcohol):** Alcohol may be the primary coping skill for this individual and it's hard for them to imagine living without it. It's important to develop other ways of coping (so you don't just rely on alcohol). You'll need a long list of **coping skills** during stressful times-and not just rely on one. Recommend using at least 20 preferred coping skills. Help develop a list of favorites and let them know that a therapist can work with them on this while they decide when they are ready to reduce their reliance on alcohol or quit drinking.

- **Moderation (Readiness):** These individuals may believe that treatment is only for those who are ready to quit drinking entirely. It's important to identify goals for drinking, whether that be abstinence or moderation. If moderation is the goal, the individual can create a **reduction plan** with a therapist and learn tricks on how to do this well. You do not need to be "ready" to quit drinking entirely to work with a therapist. They can help you "get ready."

- **Communication skills (Communicating with alcohol):** These individuals may use alcohol to escape from uncomfortable interactions with others (i.e., someone who drinks because they feel anxious in social situations; someone who drinks when they get angry in order to calm down; someone who drinks in order to smother a strong emotion). This person may be open to learning about adaptive and maladaptive communication styles. Learn how to identify them and how to effectively communicate your needs.

- **Risk analysis (Denying risk):** These individuals may not be objectively considering the risks of drinking. The goal would be to help them objectively identify the benefits and the consequences/downsides of drinking.

## COPING WITH ALCOHOL

Frequently, an individual who says they like drinking and don't want to give it up is really saying that drinking helps them deal with stress. Drinking is their preferred and primary coping skill. And let's face it, life comes with a fair amount of stress. We all have favorite coping skills. The problem comes when someone relies solely, or even mostly, on one coping skill.

To illustrate this, imagine a young mother had a really bad day. She had several angry customers at work, came home to find her washing machine had stopped working, had one child crying over a homework assignment and another refusing to eat dinner. The stress became exacerbated when she and her husband argued over how to manage the child refusing dinner. She wanted to make him macaroni and cheese; but her husband insisted that the child either eats the pork chops that were served or go to bed hungry.

Given that she was stressed from her bad day, she wanted her favorite stress reliever. Her favorite stress reliever is dancing. She is happiest when dancing.

She could choose to:

- Turn on music and dance in her house.
- Plan for a night out at the club with friends.
- Get in the car, go to a club, and start dancing.
- Spend every night for a month at a club dancing.

Whichever option she chooses comes with potential benefits and consequences. For example, choosing option d (spending the next month at clubs dancing), could make it difficult for her to manage her children, marriage, home, and work life. Likely the washing machine won't get fixed, her child won't get help doing his homework, macaroni and cheese won't be made, and ultimately none of the problems will be addressed. Additionally, it's likely it wouldn't take long for other problems to arise. By focusing so much energy engaged in dancing, her favorite coping skill, she would be neglecting opportunities to fix the problems. She would be engaged in something more like problem avoidance.

This is an example of how relying on one coping skill interferes with effectively managing life stress. To combat this, it's important to have an arsenal of coping skills. Overly relying on one causes problems, and quite frankly, we don't always have access to our favorite options. If someone's favorite coping skill is a long, hot shower, it would be difficult for them to manage stress during a work presentation while sitting in a hot shower. It's important to consider various options for coping and when stressed, choose the ones that fit the circumstance and may provide relief.

## LIST OF POTENTIAL COPING SKILLS

| | |
|---|---|
| Music | Playing with a Child |
| Art | Helping a Friend |
| Dancing | Yoga |
| Sports | Cooking |
| Praying | Eating |
| Laughing | Drinking |
| Taking a Walk | Yelling |
| Deep Breathing | Talking |
| Time in Nature | Therapy |
| Church | Venting |
| Gardening | Re-Organizing |
| Cleaning | Charity Work |
| Taking a Shower/Bath | Making a List of Options |
| Long Drives | Volunteering |
| Signing | Connecting with an Older Family Member or Friend |
| Writing | |
| Watching TV/Movies | Scrolling Social Media |
| Pets | Sleeping |

| | |
|---|---|
| Coloring | Watching the Sunset |
| Working | Watching the Sunrise |
| Sex | Photography |
| Crying | Biking |
| Shopping | Running |
| Learning a New Hobby | Working Out at the Gym |
| Fixing Something | Building Something |
| Puzzles | Massage |
| Video Games | Getting a Pedicure/Manicure |
| Bowling | Reading |
| Boating | Fishing |
| Time Near Water | Writing Down a List of Things |
| Kayaking | for Which You Are Grateful |
| Sailing | Create a List of Short-/Long- |
| Swimming | Term Goals |

It's okay to have a favorite coping skill. It's *not* okay to rely on just one. If necessary, you can work with a therapist to develop new coping skills. You can also learn tricks to reduce your reliance on one.

Exercises to consider for identifying coping skills include:

- **Ask what life would be like without alcohol.** If the answer is that alcohol is the primary method to cope with stress, consider adding other strategies in addition to alcohol. If the answer is that alcohol helps manage anxiety, please consider consulting a therapist as alcohol in the long run can make anxiety issues even worse. If the answer is that alcohol helps relax you so you can sleep, please consider consulting a therapist as alcohol can make sleep disturbance worse.

- **Identify triggers for when drinking occurs.** Be aware of when you are drinking to cope with stress.

- **Create (or have your loved one create) a list of coping skills to cope with stress.** It is okay if drinking is one of the skills on this list. If it is difficult to create this list, consider working with a therapist in order to identify and make necessary behavioral changes.

Change the thought from: **"Alcohol helps me cope with stress"** to **"Alcohol helps me cope with stress, but there are also other things that help me cope. I need more than alcohol."**

## READINESS

**You don't have to be ready to quit drinking to start treatment.** Many people indicate they are not willing to seek professional help because they believe therapists only work with people who are ready for complete and total abstinence. This is not true.

Many alcohol treatment providers work with individuals to help create a moderation or reduction plan. This helps individuals gradually reduce their drinking, perhaps at first focusing on reducing the number of nights per week where alcohol is consumed and/or reducing the number of drinks per occasion. It's important to work with a therapist and/or have a support system in place when working toward moderation because it is hard to change routines and there are several methods to help make this transition an easier one.

If you, or a loved one, is not ready to work with a professional towards reducing alcohol intake, you can join online support groups to test whether this strategy might work for you. An example of one of these groups is moderation.org.

Exercises to consider if you believe treatment means abstinence include:

- **Identify short- and long-term goals for drinking.**
- **Consider working with a therapist to meet those goals.** If ultimately the goal is abstinence, but you would like to start with a plan to reduce your drinking, identify a provider who is willing to meet you at your starting point and communicate your objectives with them.
- **Consult the resource list** (found on pages 241–242) to identify the right provider for you.

Change the thought from: **"I am not ready to quit drinking."** to **"I'm not ready to quit drinking but I might like to learn ways to reduce how much I drink."**

## COMMUNICATING WITH ALCOHOL

It's possible that the individual who says they like to drink and doesn't want to quit is saying that they don't feel comfortable communicating their own needs. Assertiveness training is a component of many alcohol treatment programs, and it is used to teach individuals how to effectively communicate their thoughts and feelings.

Imagine this scenario: Randy has been married for 15 years and has two kids. He is the manager at the town's local hardware store. He loves his job and his family and works hard to make sure he is a good provider. His own dad was not around when he was growing up and his mom worked two jobs to provide as a single mother. His mom was not affectionate, and he worried she was unhappy with him. She was neither insulting nor complimentary. He copes with stress by drinking. He drinks daily after work and routinely drinks a 12-pack every evening. His drinking increased several years ago after his mother passed away. Prior to that, he drank only on weekends and would drink a maximum of six beers per occasion. Since her death, his drinking increased in both quantity and frequency. Recently, his wife asked him if he thought he might be drinking too much, which made him feel uncomfortable. His concern is that he would be left with his own thoughts and he's not sure what to do with those thoughts and feelings.

Communication is difficult for Randy. He's not comfortable with words and prefers the routine of working and coming home to eat, drink, and sleep. Learning effective communication skills is vital for healthy relationships and healthy living. Assertiveness training is one method of teaching effective communication skills. Assertiveness training teaches how to state your needs/thoughts/feelings without violating another's needs/thoughts/feelings. Assertiveness training also teaches how to identify maladaptive communication styles such as aggressive, passive, and passive-aggressive styles. Randy would benefit from learning additional communication skills so that he does not hide behind alcohol.

Exercises to consider for the alcohol communicator include:

- Notice when you are uncomfortable stating your needs.
- Identify a therapist/provider who is willing to work on effective communication.
- Notice when communication breakdowns occur and in which context (or with whom) these breakdowns occur.

Change the thought from: **"It's hard for me to verbalize how I feel and it's easier to just drink."** to **"Maybe I can learn to identify and say how I feel."**

## DENYING RISK

It could be helpful to conduct a risk/benefit analysis to determine the impact drinking has on your life. To do this, objectively list the benefits and consequences of drinking. In order to do this effectively, it sometimes helps to have a professional or an objective individual assist in developing the list.

After formulating the list, it may be easier to recognize a path forward. Perhaps an individual will choose to seek help or they may try to cut back on their drinking or they may recognize aspects of their use that are problematic and work to avoid those particular circumstances.

Let's look at an example of a risk/benefit analysis:

**Pros**

- Taste
- Relaxation
- Celebration
- Reduces anxiety

**Cons**

- Impairs sleep
- Costs money
- People don't like me when I drink (ruins relationships)
- Blackouts
- Not good for my health
- Hard to function the next day after drinking
- Low energy

Exercises to consider if you are a risk denier include:

- Objectively list how drinking improves your life.
- Objectively list how drinking harms your life.

- If you have difficulty identifying these facts, consider consulting with a friend who is willing to be direct and honest. A therapist can also help you determine this list.

- Once you have this list, consider your goals with respect to drinking behavior for the future.

Change the thought from: **"Alcohol always helps me."** to **"There are aspects of drinking that benefit me, but it also causes some problems."**

## DAVID'S STORY REVISITED

David's story represents one individual who resisted getting treatment for alcohol use because he believed alcohol was necessary to cope with his life and that he didn't want to stop drinking. For David, the main driver behind those thoughts was that alcohol helped him cope. Drinking used to give him peace of mind and calm him down. Because he relied on alcohol to calm him down, he continued to drink. Even though it had been a while since alcohol worked to relieve his stress, he continued to believe it could work "like it used to." This is an example of David relying on alcohol to cope.

David has a long history of substance use. He began drinking in high school with a gradual uptick in use during his college years. During college, he would frequently drink 4–5 nights per week and would binge on 18–24 drinks per occasion. He continued at that rate for several years after college with it ultimately culminating in daily drinking of anywhere between 10–20 drinks per day. His first marriage ended in divorce due to his drinking and anger issues. For David's treatment to be a success, he will need to identify and use other coping skills (aside from drinking), and he may need to identify triggers for anger and methods to communicate his needs in ways that don't violate others. Further, his history with his father may be something he would like to discuss further in treatment.

In terms of coping skills, David has relied solely on alcohol to manage stress in recent years despite the reality that it has not been working for him. He used to work out regularly and this might be one tool he brings back into his life. It's critical that David identify multiple methods to manage stress and agitation.

David said it best when he said it's no longer time to justify continuing to drink. It's time for him to start justifying reasons to stop. And to do this effectively, he will need to use more effective strategies to deal with stress. Step 1 is a realistic change in his perception that he "likes" alcohol and doesn't want to give it up. The truth for David is that he liked how it used to calm him down, but it no longer provides that relief. Therefore, it is time for David to consider other methods to help him feel calm.

Consider how David's thoughts about alcohol and alcohol treatment changed and changed his behavior:

| **INITIAL THOUGHTS** |
|---|
| "I like alcohol" |
| "Alcohol tastes good and it calms my nerves" |
| "I'm not like my dad, a real alcoholic" |
| **INITIAL FEELINGS** |
| Agitated |
| Refuse to get help for alcohol |
| **INITIAL BEHAVIORS** |
| Drink |
| Yell at son |
| Break chair |
| Black out |
| **NEW THOUGHTS** |
| "My dad never got help for alcohol use and he needed it." |
| "I don't want to be like my dad." |
| "Alcohol used to calm my nerves, but it isn't working anymore." |
| "Drinking isn't working out for me very well." |
| **NEW FEELINGS** |
| Resigned |
| **NEW BEHAVIORS** |
| Call to schedule an appointment with a doctor to discuss alcohol treatment. |

# KEY SUMMARY POINTS

The main idea of this chapter focuses on the thought that some-one doesn't want to go to treatment because they like alcohol and don't want to quit drinking.

Drill down to discover what is really driving these thoughts. Possible explanations include:

- Alcohol is their primary coping skill and living without alcohol feels terrifying. Work on developing additional coping skills.

- They aren't ready to be completely abstinent, and they think they need to be before they consider treatment. Work on a reduction in use plan.

- Alcohol helps them escape from situations where they don't know how to communicate their needs to others. Work on building communication skills.

- They have not objectively considered the risks versus bene-fits of alcohol use. Conduct a risk/benefit analysis.

Once the motivation behind the statement is identified, it's easier to have an honest and realistic discussion about treatment.

## DECISION TREE

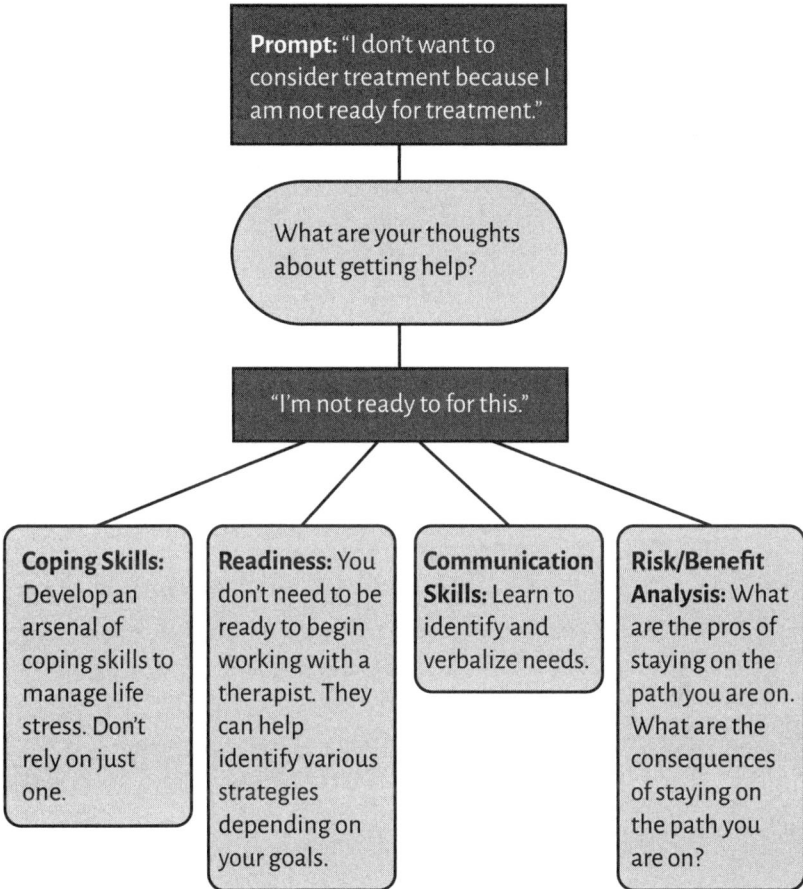

**Prompt:** "I don't want to consider treatment because I am not ready for treatment."

What are your thoughts about getting help?

"I'm not ready to for this."

**Coping Skills:** Develop an arsenal of coping skills to manage life stress. Don't rely on just one.

**Readiness:** You don't need to be ready to begin working with a therapist. They can help identify various strategies depending on your goals.

**Communication Skills:** Learn to identify and verbalize needs.

**Risk/Benefit Analysis:** What are the pros of staying on the path you are on. What are the consequences of staying on the path you are on?

# CHAPTER 8

# "WHAT ABOUT THE STIGMA?"

THIS CHAPTER HIGHLIGHTS how to talk to someone who isn't seeking help because they believe it is stigmatizing. This chapter begins using the story of Joshua to illustrate an example of how to talk to someone who is concerned about stigma. The chapter ends with suggestions for how to change someone's mind when they are worried about stigma.

## JOSHUA'S STORY: A CASE STUDY

Joshua is an 18-year-old senior in high school with a promising college career. One day he is driving down the road and a car pulls out in front of him. Joshua does not have enough time to slam on his brakes and he hits the car. The driver of the other car is a 75-year-old man who is experiencing a significant medical event, which contributed to his pulling out in front of Joshua. The driver of the other car dies at the scene of the accident from causes unrelated to the accident.

This event has a significant impact on Joshua's life and functioning. He starts isolating and spends more time in his room by himself. He has difficulty being in a car and refuses to drive. He becomes quiet and short-tempered. He has difficulty concentrating in school and his grades begin to fall. He has nightmares involving trying to save someone who is just out of reach. He starts sleeping during the day and stays awake at night. He no longer hangs out with his friends.

A year later, Joshua is still experiencing significant difficulties with his functioning and his parents are distraught because they would like for him to seek professional help and he refuses to go. His mother is worried because he is a good kid and has a promising life in front of him. He has a scholarship to his favorite college and intends to study engineering. His mother is also worried that he might be thinking of hurting himself.

When she asks him to seek help, he says:

1.  I can't believe this happened to me.

2.  I don't want to talk to anyone about what happened because they will think I killed that man.

3.  I don't want anyone to know that I sought treatment.

## WORKING THROUGH RESISTANCE TO TREATMENT

Stigma is a negative belief towards something, someone, or oneself (self-stigma). With respect to mental health, it's the act of labeling someone as "crazy" or "nuts" if they have a mental health condition. Stigma towards mental health and substance use disorders as well as mental health and substance use treatment persists and exists in almost all demographics.

The history of stigma is beyond the scope of this book, but it is important to recognize the catastrophic impact stigma has on mental health treatment seeking. Stigma impacts treatment seeking because individuals say that they can't admit to themselves or to others that they are experiencing the condition and symptoms they are experiencing. This would be comparable to someone having a broken arm and walking around saying that they can't get help because they don't want anyone to know that they broke their arm. They can't admit a broken arm to themselves or to others **for fear of rejection and non-acceptance.** Even if a broken arm is treatable, the horror of admitting to others (and oneself) is too much to bear so instead a choice is made to walk around suffering and in pain pretending the arm is not broken.

Imagine a young woman who is pregnant, but unwilling to admit to herself or others that she is pregnant. Her refusal to acknowledge her pregnancy doesn't change the reality of the pregnancy; however, it does impact how she cares for herself and her baby during the pregnancy. This is how stigma impacts mental health conditions and treatment seeking.

The next section of this chapter will focus on how stigma impacts thoughts about mental health and substance use disorders and treatment and ways that you can help someone reconsider these thoughts so that they are more likely to consider getting help. Stigma is reflected by essentially two thoughts. The first is that they don't want others to know what is happening for them and the second is that they don't want to admit it to themselves.

Someone struggling with thoughts of stigma might say things like:

- "I don't want anyone to know."
- "I can't believe this is happening to me."
- "People will think that I'm bad (or crazy or nuts)."

If you have someone in your life who is refusing treatment and saying these thoughts, there are a variety of ways to have a discussion with them to get them to reconsider these thoughts.

These include discussions about:

1.  How no one needs to know.
2.  Overcoming obstacles is cool.
3.  Underdogs are heroes.

Let's address these three points in more detail.

# CONFIDENTIALITY

### THERE IS NO "LIST"

When someone is struggling with the idea of stigma, they often believe that others "know" what is happening, as though there may be a sign on a person seeking mental health or substance use treatment. While it is true that others can sense when an individual is struggling, it is not true that others know when someone is in treatment.

Treatment is confidential. **You don't have to tell anyone that you are getting help and there is no list.** There is no list that gets published in local or national records on who is seeking treatment. There is no tattoo that gets put on your forehead that says, "TREATMENT SEEKER." There is no sign or shirt that an individual must wear when they are getting help for a mental health or substance use condition. There is no list that one can consult to gossip that Person X was in treatment for depression or anxiety or for alcohol use. In certain states, there is a list of individuals who have been flagged for serious and severe mental health conditions, but no list containing all individuals who have sought help. **There is no list.** If you don't wish for others to know you are getting help, consider not telling them.

Change the thought from: **"People will think I'm crazy if I get help."** to **"No one even needs to know that I'm getting help."** or **"I'm not myself right now and people are noticing that I'm struggling. I'd rather get help so I can get back to myself."**

## ONLINE PROVIDERS

Despite there being no list on who has received treatment (except for in confidential medical records), individuals may feel uncomfortable walking into a mental health clinic. Perhaps they live in a small town and do not want to be seen walking in. If this is the case, there are a variety of online treatment options. There are several websites to consult to decide which treatment provider is best for a specific individual. Psychologytoday.com is an excellent resource for finding local treatment providers (please see Chapter 11 for a more complete list of resources).

Change the thought from: "**I don't want anyone to see that I'm walking into a treatment center.**" to "**I can get help online and no one needs to know.**"

## CONCERNS ABOUT IMPACT TO JOB/CUSTODY

The issue of confidentiality and stigma also impacts people who believe seeking help might negatively affect their job or custody case, etc. People only know that someone is seeking help if you tell them. Otherwise, help-seeking is confidential. For the individual that is worried about negative impacts to their job or divorce or custody case, consider the possibility of how it might be perceived if you don't seek help. For example, consider the individual who is dependent on drugs. Not seeking help for their drug use could look WORSE in a custody case than actually getting help. It's important to consider the flip side of help-seeking. Those who need help but do not get it may be perceived in worse shape than someone who is trying.

Change the thought from: "**Getting help will hurt my custody case.**" to "**I'm uncomfortable admitting that I'm struggling, but I am struggling so I might as well try and get help.**" or "**Asking for help will make it look like I'm trying, and I might even start to feel better.**"

# OVERCOMING OBSTACLES IS COOL

It's not what happens to you but how you react to it that matters. We all face obstacles in life. Some are monumental while others are more manageable. Sometimes obstacles pile up all at the same time, which can feel overwhelming. Consider the number of people who have overcome obstacles. For example, professional athletes who were out of the game because of substance use issues, but who fought back and returned to their sport and triumphed (for example, Darren Walker). Professional athletes who were cut from their team, but who fought back by working hard and returned to their sport and triumphed (for example, Michael Jordan).

We all know someone who has a disease or missing limb or an emotional or cognitive limitation who doesn't live within the means of their limitation but instead moves beyond it. People who work to overcome an obstacle are cool, triumphant, and strong. It's not what happens to you that matters, but how you react to it. Yes, there are certain things that happen in life that can feel defeating and overwhelming and impossible. Perseverance and joy are possible on the other side of that pain.

Change the thought from: **"I can't overcome this."** to **"This situation is too much for me, but I won't quit. I might need help overcoming this."**

## UNDERDOGS ARE HEROES

Who doesn't love an underdog? Many of us feel a strong desire to see the underdog win. Movies have been made based on the theme of the underdog. Examples include *The Bad News Bears, Rudy, Rocky, Lord of the Rings.* **We cheer on the underdog because it is thrilling to overcome.**

Change the thought from: **"I can't believe this is happening to me."** to **"I can't believe this is happening to me but I'm going to fight on."**

# CONTINUING JOSHUA'S STORY

Joshua's mom talked with him about her concerns for his future. They discussed his love for his dog, Cooper. Joshua's family got the dog from the pound when he was about 7 months old. Cooper's original family had been charged with both child and animal abuse charges and animal control removed Cooper, his litter mates, and the puppies mother pending charges. When the adults were found guilty of the charges, Joshua's family legally adopted Cooper. Cooper was an anxious puppy. He cowered from loud noises and would try to hide. His favorite hiding spot was behind the drapes, which Joshua found endearing because he could see the big lump of puppy easily hiding behind the drapes. Cooper had severe burns on his body from abuse. Over time, Joshua watched Cooper emerge from an anxious, burned puppy into a loving, happy dog.

Joshua's mother discussed how Cooper was in bad shape when they first got him but how he overcame his fear. She asked Joshua to consider how hard it must have been for the dog to trust, but how he learned to trust through love. She told Joshua that she loved him and that she believed he would be able to move through this pain if he would try.

After this conversation with his mom, the phone rang. It was his friend, Dan. He hadn't talked to many of his friends since the accident, and he surprised himself by answering the call.

**Joshua:** Hi Dan.

**Dan:** Josh! How's it going?

**Joshua:** Okay.

**Dan:** We are getting together at Joe's. Want to meet up with us?

**Joshua:** Nah. I'm good.

**Dan:** Okay. Well, you doing okay?

**Joshua:** Fine.

**Dan:** Want to come watch the game at my house instead? We were all going to watch it at Joe's, but we could just hang at my place if that works better.

**Joshua:** I'll think about it.

**Dan:** Remember Steve Atkinson man? That dude must've weighed around 400 pounds by the time we were freshmen in high school. Remember him?

**Joshua:** His weight didn't seem to bother him. He struggled in PE though. Remember when we had to run the stairs and Mr. Kotter used to make us wait for him to finish?

**Dan:** Bro, he lost all his weight. Dude looks good.

**Joshua:** No way!

**Dan:** He does! Must weigh around 180 now. And he has a girlfriend!

**Joshua:** Laughs. That's great to hear. I'm happy for him.

**Dan:** Atkinson, man. Love to watch the underdog overcome.

**Joshua:** My mom was just talking to me about Cooper and how scared he was when we first got him.

**Dan:** I was coming over there for 2-3 years before he'd let me pet him.

**Joshua:** Yeah.

**Dan:** Cool how he overcame all of that.

**Joshua:** Yeah. It is cool.

**Dan:** I know you went through something hard too. You ever think about getting help?

**Joshua:** My mom was just talking to me about getting help, but I don't know. I know everyone knows what happened, but I don't want anyone to know. And I wouldn't want anyone to know that I got help.

**Dan:** Josh. No one thinks the accident was your fault. That man had a stroke while driving. There was nothing you could do. It wasn't anybody's fault.

**Joshua:** I haven't been able to talk about it. I still can't believe it happened. I worry about what people are saying.

**Dan:** Everyone is saying that it was awful and miss you. No one thinks bad of you.

**Joshua:** Ha. Maybe I can join Cooper and Atkinson.

**Dan:** And overcome. Everyone loves the person who can overcome a bad situation.

**Joshua:** Would be nice to overcome these bad feelings. If Cooper can do it, I can do it.

**Dan:** Bro. If Atkinson can overcome, you can overcome. You got this.

Joshua asked his mom to help him schedule an appointment with a psychologist because he wanted to be like Steve and Cooper and work through his overwhelming feelings of guilt and shame.

## OVERCOMING STIGMA

Joshua is having a hard time after a traumatic car accident that resulted in the death of another person. Joshua experiences nightmares and avoids people, places, and things that remind him of the accident. He is isolating and no longer engaging in social or school activities. Joshua is exhibiting symptoms of PTSD. Treatment for PTSD could help Joshua process his thoughts and feelings about the accident and find meaning.

Joshua changes his perspective about seeking help during a phone call with his friend Dan. Dan asks Joshua his thoughts about getting help and Joshua states that he doesn't want anyone to know about what happened or that he got help. Dan helps Joshua see that 1) everyone already knows, and 2) no one is judging him negatively, 3) his friends want him around, and 4) it would be perceived as cool to overcome this (just like their friend overcame his struggle with weight). Joshua is able to relate this to his conversation with his mom earlier that day highlighting how his dog also overcame a traumatic experience. Joshua's thought about seeking help changed during this conversation. Joshua's initial thoughts were:

| INITIAL THOUGHTS |
|---|
| "I can't believe this happened to me. |
| "I don't want to talk to anyone about what happened." |
| "I don't want anyone to know that I sought treatment." |

| INITIAL FEELINGS |
|---|
| Depressed |
| Defeated |
| Ashamed |

| INITIAL BEHAVIORS |
|---|
| Isolates |
| Does not seek help |
| After this discussion with Dan, Joshua's thoughts changed to: |

| NEW THOUGHTS |
|---|
| "I can't believe this happened to me, but I need help." |
| "It's hard to talk about what happened, but I need to try. For Cooper." |
| "I want everyone to know that even though I was struggling,<br>I worked through the sadness and overcame." |

| NEW FEELINGS |
|---|
| Hopeful |

| NEW BEHAVIORS |
|---|
| Asks his mom to schedule an appointment |

# KEY SUMMARY POINTS

The main idea of this chapter is that people don't seek help because they are worried about stigma and others knowing that they are struggling.

Strategies to overcome these thoughts include:

1. No one needs to know that you are getting help. Help is confidential.

2. Overcoming obstacles is cool.

3. Underdogs are heroes.

## DECISION TREE

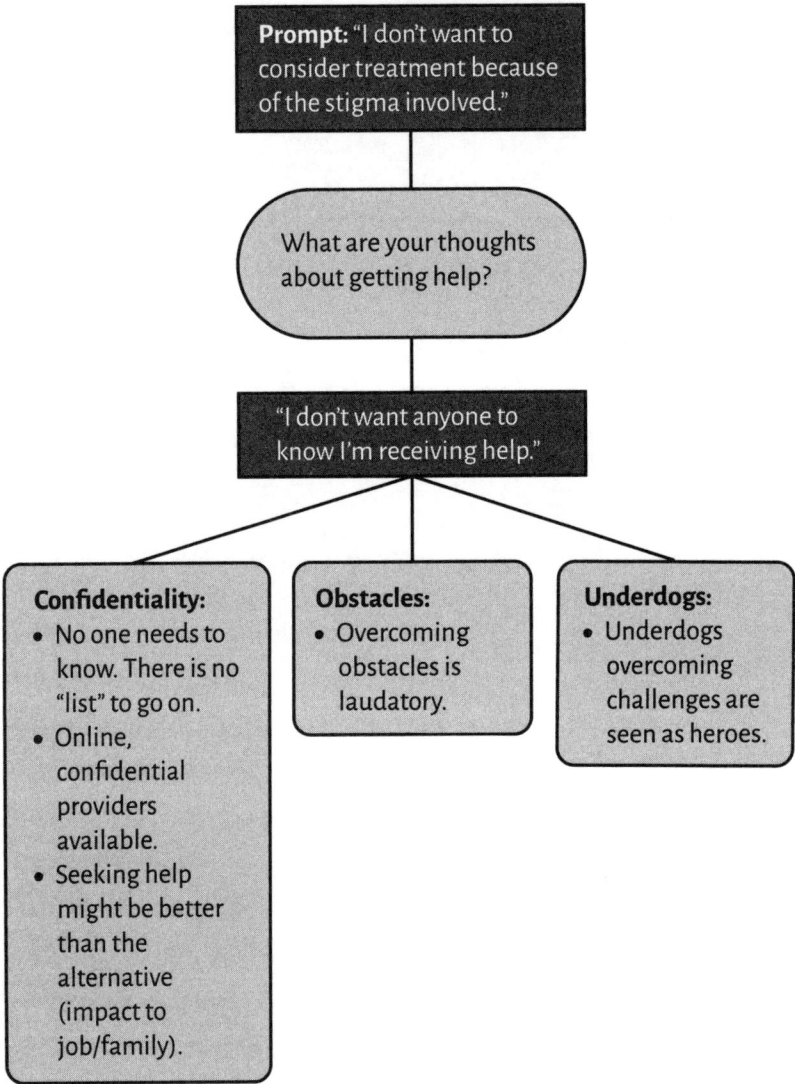

**Prompt:** "I don't want to consider treatment because of the stigma involved."

What are your thoughts about getting help?

"I don't want anyone to know I'm receiving help."

**Confidentiality:**
- No one needs to know. There is no "list" to go on.
- Online, confidential providers available.
- Seeking help might be better than the alternative (impact to job/family).

**Obstacles:**
- Overcoming obstacles is laudatory.

**Underdogs:**
- Underdogs overcoming challenges are seen as heroes.

# CHAPTER 9

# "I DON'T NEED HELP"

**T**HIS CHAPTER HIGHLIGHTS how to talk to someone who isn't seeking help because they believe they don't need help. The chapter starts with the story of Dillon, presented both from Dillon's perspective and his provider's perspective. It is offered as an example of how to talk to someone who believes they don't need help. The chapter ends with suggestions for how to change someone's mind who has this thought.

## DILLON'S STORY: A CASE STUDY

The last thing I need in my life right now is to be sitting in a damn doctor's office with a broken arm. Get me out of here.

"Hi. Can you tell me what brings you in today?" a young guy says as he walks in to see me.

"Got in a fight."

"Okay. Where does it hurt?"

I point to my arm, and he says, "Can you show me specifically where you are experiencing pain and tell me what happened?"

"I was fighting this guy and ran into a car."

"Anywhere else on your body you're feeling pain? Where did the car hit you? Did you hit your head?"

"No. I didn't hit my head." I hit the other guy's head on the street multiple times, but the doctor doesn't need to know that. "The car came out of nowhere and I rolled over the hood. My arm is the only thing that hurts."

"Alright, I'm going to order x-rays and we can look at what is going on."

"How long will this take?"

"Shouldn't take more than a couple minutes to get the x-rays. I'll have the nurse in here in a minute to take you to get them done."

I don't want to be here. I wouldn't be here at all except seeing that asshole this morning made me want to punch him in the face. So I did. Why did that damn car have to come around the corner right then? At least the nurse comes in quick to get x-rays done and get me out of here, but the doctor takes forever to come back to the room. When the doctor comes back, he says, "Okay, I've looked at your x-rays." He pulls up his computer screen and points to them. I see a bone and I can tell that it's broken. He points to the break and says, "You have a fracture in your humerus. I don't think it's severe enough to require surgery, but you will need a cast and a splint."

He tells me that the cast is a full arm, up the shoulder so this is going to take a while. He asks if I'm in pain. I shrug.

"Do you live with someone? Anyone around to help you out for the next couple of months? You're going to need some help." He asks.

"I live with my parents," I say.

"Would you like me to call them?" he asks.

"No." God no.

Damn. This hurts. Hope the pain meds come soon.

I can feel him staring at me when he says, "You must be in so much pain." I look him in the eye and think that no one has ever asked about my pain before, including me. "I'm fine."

"Okay, well I can get pain meds for you and set up a psych consult if you'd like."

"The fuck would I want a psych consult?" I yell.

"Not saying you want one, just saying I can set one up."

"No."

"Up to you whether you schedule an appointment with psych, but I'd like to do a referral anyway. Seems you could use a little help. And you look to be in more pain than you are letting on which leads me to believe you are used to hiding pain," he goes on about counselors. Counselors? For fuck's sake. What would a counselor do?

"I hate counselors," I tell him.

"Oh? Worked with counselors before?"

"When I was a kid. At school."

"What would you talk about?" he asks.

None of your fucking business. "Nothing."

"What did you want to talk to them about?" he asks.

That I hated my dad, hated being at home, hated my life. "I hated school. And I hate counselors."

"Oh. I didn't like school either," he says.

"You don't look like you hated school." He looks like a kid who *loved* school. The kid who got excited about new pencils, markers, and notebooks. He looks like the kid who sat in the front of the classroom and actually listened to teachers. The kind of kid who had a mom that made peanut butter and jelly sandwiches and homemade chocolate chip cookies for his lunches and brought in homemade cupcakes to the classroom every year when it was his birthday. The kind of kid who had a mom that picked him up from school instead of making him ride the bus home to an empty house. This kid didn't have a dad who used him as a punching bag and made him sleep outside whenever he had "business" to attend (often) or used him as a pawn in some business deal (terrifying).

The doctor continues, "I did *not* like school despite how I look. I had my own things to deal with. How about your parents? Sounds like you are close with them considering you live with them."

Is this guy for real? "No. We are not close." We are not close at all. My mom is a zombie, either drugged out or dancing. She is gentle. But damaged. She's not strong enough to deal with my dad, so spends most of her time drugged out. "Mom was okay."

"Dad not so much? Listen you seem like you have some stuff to deal with so I'll leave you with a referral to psych. I know you didn't like counseling when you were young, but you're older now and are free to talk about whatever is on your mind."

"I don't need help," I tell him.

"What does that mean that you don't need help?"

"Means I don't need help."

"Everybody needs help. What does it mean to you to need help?" he prods.

"Means you are weak," I tell him.

"Oh. Well. You came here to get help with your arm," he replies.

"Weak," I tell him.

"Breaking an arm is *painful*. You think it's weak to reset bones so they can heal properly? It doesn't seem weak to me. It seems smart. Emotional pain is no different. You injured your brain, just like your arm. You come in for your arm, you can come in for your brain."

"No," I tell him.

"Any reason you want to keep suffering?"

"Just don't need to talk about things."

"You don't *need* to talk about things? What would happen if you did talk about things?" he asks me while he shows me how to apply the sling so that my shoulder will stay put.

What he doesn't understand is that talking will make things *worse*. My dad always said to keep my mouth shut. I'm not allowed to talk. Even my attorney told me to shut up. How could a counselor help?

On the other hand, I bet nobody ever told this doctor to shut up. Seems some people are allowed to talk all they want. They talk all day long. About everything. To everyone! I've watched those people my whole life. Wonder why they're allowed to talk and I'm not? Maybe I'd have been better off if I had talked to someone when I was a kid. Maybe if I had said something somewhere along the way someone would've stepped in to help? I'm an adult now but I was just a kid back then. Maybe it would've helped if I had talked to the counselor? I was too scared to say anything back then. I'm not sure I'm scared anymore.

What would happen if I did talk to someone?

*I don't know because I've never tried. I was always told to shut my mouth.*

Are things better because I shut up?

*No. Things are worse than ever.*

Where did I learn to shut up?

*My dad.*

"What could a counselor do to help me anyway?" I ask him.

"That's a good question. I think the answer depends on you. What would you want to work on?" he asks.

"I'm in trouble with the law. Nothing is working out and everyone pisses me off. I'm not even allowed to talk to anyone." I tell him.

"You're talking to me. Seems like we are doing okay. Who told you you weren't allowed to talk to people?" he asks me.

I look back at him and don't respond.

"Okay. You were told that you weren't allowed to talk. In my experience, people who tell you not to say anything are protecting themselves more than they are protecting you. The question is whether or not you agree. How bad has it been talking to me?"

"You're okay. Kinda."

"Lots of people like me you can talk to. Maybe consider whether staying silent has benefited you. You said you're in trouble. Being in trouble and alone may be worse than talking to someone. How bad does it need to get before you ask for help?"

It's hard for me to imagine right now, but this doc has a point. Things suck and nothing is going right. Maybe it can't hurt to talk to someone. I don't think things could get any worse.

## DILLON'S DOCTOR'S STORY

A rotation in emergency medicine as a first-year medical resident is eye-opening. We go through a variety of rotations during first-year, like ob-gyn, internal medicine, emergency medicine, psych, etc. I like all of them, but my favorite is probably psych. My least favorite is surgery because it's hard to stand for 5 hours straight.

I enjoy talking to patients and prefer when the patient is able to participate in the discussion.

I'm not sure how I feel about this rotation in emergency medicine, although I enjoyed my last patient. He was a 5-year-old white male who presented with increased thirst and hunger, increased urination, and weight loss. He was calm and articulate. I consulted with my attending, ran blood work, and got his A1C. A diagnosis of Type 1 Diabetes as a child is traumatic, although the family seemed equipped to support him. The parents were concerned and asked for appropriate support services. They will need them. I'm not sure they understand the beast of diabetes they are about to meet.

On our surgery rotation, we learned not to mess with the pancreas and this child's pancreas is not working. We also learned that every patient is a psych patient. My parents would not have been able to manage a chronic illness like diabetes. My mom had her own issues that consumed her, so it's nice to see this little boy is from a family that could help him.

My next patient is a 25-year-old white male who presented to the ED with arm pain. The nurse reported he refused to say much while she was doing vitals and to be wary of a potential head injury. I'll have her stay in the room with me as per protocol while I conduct my evaluation in case he becomes combative. I've never had a patient become violent, but my guess is I'll see it at some point this year. Okay, here we go.

"Hi. Can you tell me what brings you in today?"

"Got in a fight."

"Okay. Where does it hurt?"

He points to his arm, and I say, "Can you show me specifically where you are experiencing pain and tell me what happened?"

Whoa. I think I know this patient. I saw a news story on him a couple weeks ago. The news said he's been charged with assault on a minor. The story said he has multiple assault charges against him including one against a child. He also has a charge of animal abuse. This is not someone I expected to see in the ED. Maybe it's not him, but someone that looks like him? Either way, I'll focus on this patient and not get caught up in anything other than patient care.

"I was fighting this guy and ran into a car."

Okay, this may, in fact, be the guy on the news story. He seems to like to fight.

"Anywhere else on your body you are feeling pain? Where did the car hit you? Did you hit your head?"

"I didn't hit my head. The car came out of nowhere and I rolled over the hood. My arm is the only thing that hurts."

"Alright, I'm going to order x-rays and we can take a look at what is going on."

"How long will this take?"

"Shouldn't take more than a couple minutes to get the x-rays. I'll have the nurse in here in a minute to take you to get them done."

X-rays are conclusive. Fracture of the humerus. Check in with my attending who confirms treatment as a cast and splint. Let my attending know that the patient has various charges against him (confirmed by google). The attending comes in the room with me to give the patient the diagnosis and treatment, but he leaves me to do the cast on my own.

Wonder what happened to him that he would do that to a kid? And a dog? My job is to put on the cast. The judicial system can sort out the rest.

The cast is a full arm, up the shoulder so I'll be with him for a while. He's not chatty and we sit in silence. I ask about his pain and he grunts that he is fine. This break would be pretty painful and he's grimacing, so I know he's not fine. Maybe he's experienced pain before in his life a time or two. I offer and order pain meds for him.

"Do you live with someone? Anyone around to help you out for the next couple of months? You're going to need some help," I tell him.

"I live with my parents," he replies.

"Would you like me to call them?" I ask.

"No."

Wonder what his parents are like? It's good to be objective and stick to the facts because sometimes the facts of the case are surprising and not what you're expecting. Facts for this patient. He is a 25-year-old white male with a fractured humerus upon impact with a moving vehicle. Vitals unremarkable. Lives with parents. Hygiene acceptable. Contusions on face and hand, some visible swelling. Oriented to time and place. Additional information would include that he's not interested in talking and has multiple criminal charges against him unrelated to his current medical visit.

Personally, I feel a strong compulsion to finish up with him and move on to my next patient. It's difficult to be in the room with him, although I'm not sure why I feel that way. I like most people, it's just that he reminds me of when I used to visit my mom when she was hospitalized. Visits with her in the hospital were awful. I loved seeing her and needed to hug her, but she was surrounded by people that felt dangerous. I wanted to protect her, and I couldn't. My grandma would pull me away at the end of the visits and I didn't want to leave my mom there alone. The other people made me feel weird and unsafe. This guy makes me feel unsafe. Being in the room with him reminds me of how I felt when I would leave my mom at the hospital.

The patient grimaces again as I manipulate his arm.

"You must be in so much pain." As I say this to him, I can feel the energy in the room change. He makes eye contact with me for the first time.

"I'm fine," he says even though he's clearly not fine.

"Okay, well I can get pain meds for you and set up a psych consult if you'd like."

"The fuck would I want a psych consult?" he yells.

"Not saying you want one, just saying I can set one up."

"No."

Silence. I work on his cast and wonder why I even offered to schedule a psych consult. He clearly was not going to accept it. The only thing I can figure is that I see psychological pain, so I offer a psych consult. Probably shouldn't explain that to him though.

"Up to you whether you schedule an appointment with psych, but I'd like to do a referral anyway," I explain even as I just told myself that I don't need to explain it to him. Anyone who is getting into fights and running into cars seems like someone who might need some help. "Seems you could use a little help. And you seem to be in more pain than you are letting on, which leads me to believe you are used to hiding pain." Maybe no one has ever acknowledged his pain.

He's not looking at me when he says, "I hate counselors."

"Oh? Worked with counselors before?" I ask.

"When I was a kid. At school."

"What would you talk about?" I ask.

"Nothing."

"What did you want to talk to them about?" I ask him.

He looks at me, glaring. "I hated school. And I hate counselors."

"Oh. I didn't like school either," I tell him.

"You don't look like you hated school."

Laugh. I did hate school although it's fair that he said that. I look like a nerd. "I did not like school despite how I look. I had my own things to deal with." I tell him, remembering what it was like to be at school when I was worried about my mom. "How about your parents? Sounds like you are close with them considering you live with them."

"Not really," he replies and then several minutes go by as I finish up his cast. Then he says, "Mom was okay."

"Dad not so much?" I ask.

Again, he looks me in the eyes but does not reply. Okay, so perhaps dad isn't a great guy. No surprise really considering the news story I watched the other night. He beat a child and threw a dog into traffic. "Listen you seem like you have some stuff to deal with so I'll leave you with a referral to psych. I know you didn't like counselors when you were young, but you're older now and are free to talk about whatever is on your mind."

"I don't need help," he says.

"Everybody needs help. What does that mean that you don't need help?" I ask him because he seems exactly like someone who could use a little help.

"Means I don't need help."

"What does it mean to you to need help?" I ask him.

"Means you are weak," he replies.

"Oh. Well. You came here to get help with your arm," I tell him.

He laughs and says, "Weak."

"Breaking an arm is *painful*. You think it's weak to reset bones so they can heal properly? It doesn't seem weak to me. It seems smart. Emotional pain is no different. You injured your brain, just like your arm. You come in for your arm, you can come in for your brain."

"No," he tells me.

"Any reason you want to keep suffering?"

"Just don't need to talk about things."

"You don't *need* to talk about things? What would happen if you did talk about things?"

Silence, so I show him how to apply the sling so that his shoulder will stay put allowing the bone time to heal.

"What could a counselor do to help me anyway?" he asks me.

"That's a good question. I think the answer depends on you. What would you want to work on?" I ask him.

"I'm in trouble with the law. Nothing is working out and everyone pisses me off. I'm not even allowed to talk to anyone," he states.

"You're talking to me. Seems like we are doing okay. Who told you you weren't allowed to talk to people?" I ask.

I get the pointed look again, but no response.

"Okay. You were told that you weren't allowed to talk. In my experience, people who tell you not to say anything are protecting themselves more than they are protecting you. The question is whether or not you agree. How bad has it been talking to me?"

"You're okay. Kinda."

"Lots of people like me you can talk to. Maybe consider whether staying silent has benefitted you. You said you're in trouble. Being in trouble and alone may be worse than talking to someone. How bad does it need to get before you ask for help?"

We wrap up and I let him know that the nurse will be in with instructions on caring for his cast and a referral.

## WORKING THROUGH RESISTANCE TO TREATMENT

One of the most common reasons individuals say they don't want to get help for mental health and substance use disorders is, "I don't need help." In their opinion, they do not have a problem and do not need help. It is possible that they don't need help; however, it is a different situation when someone is struggling at work, school, socially, legally, financially, with their health, or in family situations (and especially if struggling in all of these). This is when it is important to consider objective criteria for defining the need for help. The next section of this chapter will focus on how to have conversations with individuals who believe they don't need help for a mental health or substance use issue; and ways to help someone reconsider so they are more likely to consider getting help.

Someone arguing that they don't need help might say things like:

- I don't need help.
- I'm doing okay just the way I am.
- Everyone *else* is the problem; *I'm* fine.

Strategies to help someone consider treatment who insist they "don't need help" include:

1.  Identify what it means to that individual to "need" help.

    o   Step 1: Identify what it means to need help.

    o   Step 2: Understand where they learned that thought.

    o   Step 3: Consider other perspectives.

2.  Identify a reality-based concrete bottom line for when you will need help.

3.  Consider the consequences of current functioning.

## DEFINE "NEEDING HELP"

It's frustrating when someone is struggling, but they say they don't need help. What do you say to someone who clearly needs help, but they say they don't? They might not be seeing their situation clearly so **it's important to focus on concrete and objective facts.**

Objectively, you identify someone as functioning poorly if they have impairment socially, occupationally (work or school), or physically. Social impairment might mean they have friction with others, are isolating, and/or do not have quality relationships with others. Occupational impairment might mean they are not performing well at work or school (absent or unproductive). Physical impairment might mean they are tired, have no interest in engaging in activities, or are unable to physically engage in activities. If any of these three types of impairment exist because of a mental health or substance use problem, seeking help could be useful.

| FUNCTIONAL IMPAIRMENT | |
| --- | --- |
| **SOCIAL** | Poor social relationships |
| **OCCUPATIONAL** | Poor functioning at work or school |
| **PHYSICAL** | Poor physical or emotional health |

Here is a three-step process to help guide discussions with an individual who needs help but says they don't.

## A THREE-STEP PROCESS

1.  Understand what "need help" means to that person.

2.  Understand the extent to which they believe their thoughts are true/accurate.

3.  If their thoughts are not true, what is true?

## STEP 1: UNDERSTAND WHAT "NEED HELP" MEANS TO THAT PERSON

To need help means different things to different people. For some people, asking for help is easy. For other people, it's easy to ask for help on certain things but hard on other aspects of their lives. And for some people, asking for help *on anything* is akin to wanting to jump into a pit of steaming hot tar. Step 1 is to ask that person what they mean when they say that they don't need help.

Below is a list of common reasons why people state they don't need help. Understanding what someone means when they say that they don't need help is essential for productive and effective conversations to happen. Ask them what *they* mean when they say they don't need help. It might be difficult to resist the urge to tell them your opinion of their need for help, but to understand their perspective, yours should not be part of the conversation.

On a side note, when asking someone what they mean when they say that they don't need help, it's important to make sure that you are genuinely interested in *their* response. It might seem as though they are being stubborn and denying what is going on, but it's probably not that. There are people who refuse to acknowledge any problem or that there is any reasonable solution or treatment for that problem, but most people who state that they don't need help are not being obstinate. Instead, they have a belief that is in the way of them getting help. Talking it through with them with a genuine interest in understanding how they are thinking and what drives the thought is helpful in the long run. It may even be surprising what you learn about each other in these conversations. Come to the conversation ready to talk *and* to learn.

A list of possible reasons why people believe they don't need help might include:

- Getting help is for the **weak**.
- Might need help but only if the problem is severe. It's **not bad enough** to get help.
- There is nothing that anyone can do to help with the problem. It **won't work**.

- Would require work/effort to get help and **not ready to put in the effort**.

- **Embarrassed** about the situation.

- They perceive the problem to be the fault of others. **Others are really the problem**.

- **Trust issues**. They don't trust feeling vulnerable talking to others about an issue or don't trust that anyone else will really want to help them.

- Truly believe that **they do not have a problem**.

Bottom line, find out from that person what "needing help" means to them. Someone might tell you that when they were a kid they learned to never ask for help. It was something only the weak would do. They learned to be uncomfortable asking for help. Someone else might tell you that they don't need help because they don't believe anyone would really care or be able to help them. This doesn't actually mean that they don't "need" help, but instead that they have difficulty trusting someone to work with them. The only way to move forward is to understand how they think.

## STEP 2: UNDERSTAND THE EXTENT OF THEIR BELIEF

Once you understand what needing help means to that person, it's time for Step 2. In Step 2, the conversation turns to learning how they came to believe that thought.

You might ask the following questions:

- Where did they learn that thought?
- Is there evidence for/against that thought?
- How true is the thought?
- Do they apply this same thought to other people that they know? If not, under what circumstances does the thought change?
- What is the cost of having that thought? What is the benefit of having that thought?

These conversations can go in multiple directions. Let's go through examples of how this might look.

### EXAMPLE 1: DILLON

When Dillon's doctor asked him his thoughts on seeking counseling, Dillon stated that he didn't need help. He believed he didn't need help despite being in trouble legally, physically, and emotionally. When his doctor asked him what "needing help" meant to him, Dillon replied that needing help was 1) weak and 2) that he's not allowed to talk. A discussion on whether it was weak to seek help for physical (broken bone) and emotional (anger, agitation) occurred which resulted in Dillon considering changing his thought about seeking help.

**Step 1: What are your thoughts on seeking help?**

- **Dillon:** "I don't need help."

**Step 2: What does needing help mean to you?**

- **Dillon:** "It's weak."

- They explored whether it was weak to seek help for physical/ emotional issues.

- They explored whether he is allowed to "talk" to others and where he learned this thought.

## EXAMPLE 2: PAUL

Another example is Paul who grew up in a violent home. Paul's father was abusive, and he feared for his mother's life on several occasions. He grew up believing that people are not safe and avoids interactions with anyone except a trusted few. He works as an IT specialist for a company that allows him to work from home. He does well at work but will not attend work meetings. He has a girlfriend he would like to marry someday but refuses to attend any of her family functions. He experiences anxiety at the thought of in-person interactions. He has disturbed sleep and nightmares when confronted with opportunities for social interaction. From his perspective, he is thriving in work and socially.

His mother and girlfriend have told him that they would like him to attend family functions and talk with people outside of his small network. They asked him to seek help for anxiety. He does not want to go to treatment because he "doesn't need help." When his girlfriend asked him what he means when he says he doesn't need help, he responded that he thinks he is doing well at work and in his relationship and is not ready to interact with anyone else. When she asked what it meant for him to be "not ready," he admitted that he can't sleep and has nightmares when he is asked to go to her family's house for dinner and he is not ready to confront these feelings.

For Paul, the thought that he doesn't need help means that he is not ready to confront difficult memories and feelings that may be explored in therapy. Paul's girlfriend can gently ask how he came to believe that he is not ready, whether there is any evidence that this is true that he is not ready, or whether he would apply that same thought to others in similar situations.

For instance, if his mother was struggling with anxiety, would he want her to have nightmares and disturbed sleep or would he want her to consider seeking help from a professional? She may ask him to weigh the pros and cons of believing he is not ready to seek help. When would the costs of this thought start to outweigh the benefits? What if he would love his girlfriends' family, but his anxiety is holding him back from this discovery? He may not be considering some of the benefits of seeking help including learning how to react/respond in various social settings and scenarios. Creating a small, safe, and contained social and work network has been how he has managed so far, and it has worked well for him to this point. His family believes it may be time to work on his anxiety so that he can interact more fully in the world.

**Step 1: What are your thoughts on seeking help?**

- **Paul:** I don't need help.

**Step 2: What does needing help mean to you?**

- **Paul:** He thinks he's doing well.

- He's not ready to confront feeling anxiety when interacting with others.

Both of the above are examples of how to talk with someone about their thoughts on needing help.

# STEP 3: IF THE THOUGHT IS NOT FULLY TRUE OR HELPFUL, WHAT *IS* HELPFUL?

At this point in the three-step process, you know that someone isn't seeking help because they believe they don't need help and the reasons why they say they don't need help. Step 3 is where you see if there is any potential for changing that thought.

If you are talking with someone and they state, "I don't need help because my situation isn't bad enough to seek treatment. At least I still function at my job," test the "truth" of this thought. Let's say you ask them how true their thought is, and they say it is 100 percent true. It might be true that they are still functioning at their job. What might also be true is that their family relationships or other important social relationships are not doing as well. Perhaps their health or their optimism for life is poor. Take in the whole picture and help them see the bigger context. If they are indeed functioning well socially, and at work, and with their health, then perhaps they don't need help. If they are having significant impairment in one or more of these areas, then consider the overall big picture.

Changing someone's way of thinking requires:

- A discussion about their perspective.
- Open communication between the two (or more) parties.
- Authentic, respectful, empathic, active listening (see Chapter 1).
- Acceptance of their strategy to manage their life.

Remember these questions to engage in a conversation about how they view seeking help:

- Where did they learn that thought?
- Is there evidence for/against that thought?
- How true is the thought?
- Do they apply this same thought to other people that they know? If not, under what circumstances does the thought change?
- What is the cost of having that thought? What is the benefit of having that thought?

Once you've discussed their thoughts more fully, ask them if their original thought is still true. Perhaps they have changed their way of thinking. For example, the thought, "I don't need help because only a weak person asks for help" might change to something like, "I am uncomfortable asking for help but there are times when it is okay."

Overall, the three-step process for guiding a discussion when someone says that they don't need help is:

1.  Understand what "needing help" means to that person.

2.  Understand the extent to which their thought is true.

3.  If their thoughts are not true/helpful, what is true.

## DILLON'S STORY REVISITED

While the story did not document details of his abuse history, Dillon suffered from severe childhood physical abuse and neglect. To cope, Dillon distanced himself from others and resorted to violence in response to conflict. During the medical visit, Dillon's doctor talked with him about his thoughts on seeing a mental health specialist/counselor.

**Step 1: What are your thoughts on seeking help?**

- **Dillon:** "I don't need help."

**Step 2: What does needing help mean to you?**

- **Dillon:** "It's weak."
- Discussion on whether seeking help for a broken arm and seeking help for an injured brain are similar.
- Discussion on whether he is *allowed* to "talk" to others and where he learned this thought.

**Step 3: How true is it that seeking help is weak and he's not allowed to talk?**

- He was able to seek help for a broken arm, maybe he could seek help for his anger.

- He was able to have a discussion with his doctor about seeking help and didn't feel weak.

- He considered whether talking to a counselor as a kid might have actually helped his situation. Not saying anything didn't actually help.

Let's consider Dillon's initial thoughts/feelings:

| INITIAL THOUGHTS |
| --- |
| "I don't need help." |
| "Getting help is for the weak." |
| "I'm not allowed to talk." |
| **INITIAL FEELINGS** |
| Anger |
| Agitated |
| Isolated |
| **INITIAL BEHAVIORS** |
| Getting into fights, hurting children and animals, breaking bones |
| Dillon's thoughts/feelings after talking with his doctor on seeking help: |

| NEW THOUGHTS |
| --- |
| "I'm in trouble." |
| "I came in for help with this arm, maybe I can talk to a counselor." |
| "Maybe if I had talked to the counselor earlier, someone could've stepped in to help me? What if talking to someone could help?" |

| NEW FEELINGS |
| --- |
| Curious |

| NEW BEHAVIORS |
| --- |
| Considering scheduling an appointment to talk with the counselor the doctor referred him to. |

# CONSIDER A REALITY-BASED BOTTOM LINE FOR WHEN HELP WILL BE NEEDED

If someone doesn't believe that they need help, what is their bottom line for when they *would* need help? What is their perception of "rock bottom?" Ask them to identify a reality-based concrete bottom line for when help is needed. This is the point at which someone might consider seeking help if their way of handling it is no longer working. This point (or rock bottom) is specific to each individual.

Is it when they...

- Lose their job?

- Have a significant break up?

- End up in jail?

- Become hospitalized?

- Can't pay their mortgage or rent?

- Fight with friends or colleagues?

- Have a health crisis?

While it's important to know the point at which someone would consider themselves as hitting rock bottom, it's also critical to help identify next steps if they do hit rock bottom. Perhaps someone does not want to seek help, but they would be open to it if they lost their job, for example. You can help them define and verbalize their rock bottom and help them identify their Plan B. If they hit their designated bottom line point, would they be open to seeking treatment then? Help them determine their next steps. Having this identified in advance is helpful, as none of us really think all that clearly in the midst of a crisis.

| DEFINE YOUR BOTTOM LINE | |
|---|---|
| Define their perception of rock bottom | Example: Losing a job |
| Define plan for seeking help if they hit rock bottom | Example: Seeking treatment |

# CONSIDER THE CONSEQUENCES OF CURRENT FUNCTIONING

Another way to approach an individual who does not want to seek mental health or substance use treatment is to have them take an honest assessment of their current functioning.

Describe how well they are functioning:

- Socially (with friends, family, colleagues)
- Financially
- Legally
- Health (fatigue, weight loss/gain, sleeping too much or too little, pain)
- Occupationally or at school
- Emotionally (mood, loss of interest, sad, agitated or angry)
- Spiritually (loss of faith, apathy)

It's possible that an individual has not considered how well they are doing. We can all remember times when it felt like we were in survival mode. During this mode of functioning, you're only trying to get through each day as it comes. The big picture is too much to contemplate when you're really on an hour-to-hour or day-to-day basis of functioning. In these instances, you could help someone take a moment to look at the big picture and consider how well they are doing overall. It might be painful (and overwhelming) to take a step back and look at the overall picture, but also important.

Exercises to consider include:

- Write down how well you are doing (physically, emotionally, financially, etc.).
- Take a step back and consider the big picture in terms of functioning.

- If you are doing well in multiple aspects of your life, perhaps you are correct in that you don't need help! If, however, you notice problem areas it might be worthwhile considering seeking help.

Changing thought from: **"I don't need help."** to **"I thought I was doing okay, but maybe I'm struggling more than I realized."**

## KEY SUMMARY POINTS

The main idea of this chapter is that people don't seek help because they believe they don't need help.

Strategies to overcome these thoughts include:

1. Defining what "needing help" means to them.
2. Exploring whether their thought is accurate/true.
3. Consider concrete bottom line for seeking help.
4. Consider overall functioning.

## DECISION TREE

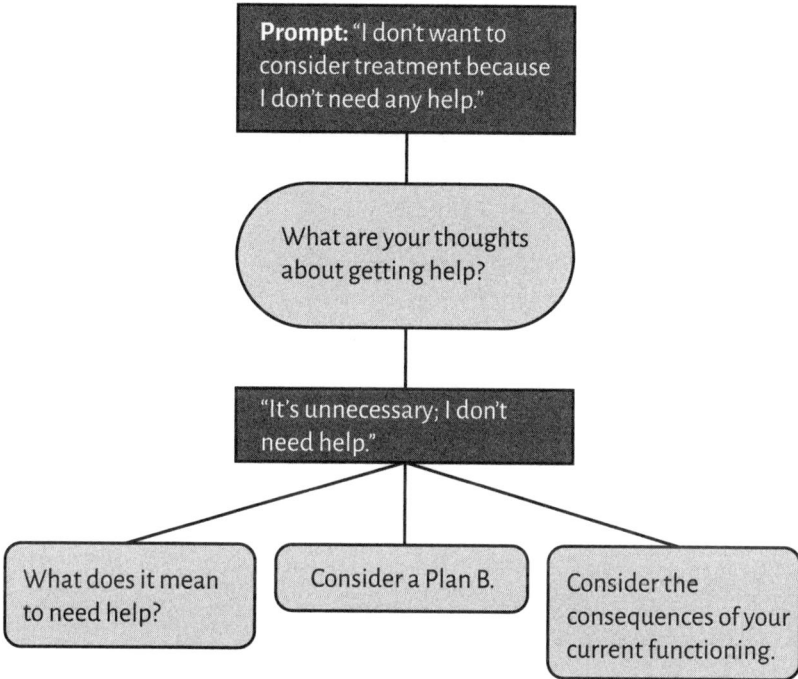

**Prompt:** "I don't want to consider treatment because I don't need any help."

What are your thoughts about getting help?

"It's unnecessary; I don't need help."

What does it mean to need help?

Consider a Plan B.

Consider the consequences of your current functioning.

# CHAPTER 10

# "THERE'S NO TIME OR MONEY FOR TREATMENT"

**T**HIS CHAPTER HIGHLIGHTS how to talk to someone who isn't seeking help because they believe they don't have time or money for treatment. The chapter starts with the story of Jack and Phoebe to illustrate an example of how to talk to someone who believes this thought. The chapter ends with suggestions for how to change someone's mind when they have this thought.

## JACK AND PHOEBE'S STORY: A CASE STUDY

I can't breathe. *"Oh my God, oh my God, oh my God. Tell me he did not do this again. Please God no."*
*[Phoebe calls her best friend Olivia.]*

**Olivia:** Hi!

**Phoebe:** Oh my God. I need to talk!

**Olivia:** What's going on?

**Phoebe:** Ollie, I could kill him.

**Olivia:** What did he do?

**Phoebe:** I got a notification on my phone just now that our rent check bounced.

**Olivia:** NO!

**Phoebe:** YES! You know how I spent Saturday night in Charlotte at Toby's soccer tournament? He must've placed bets all weekend! College football games on Saturday and then NFL games on Sunday. No wonder he volunteered to stay home with Carlie instead of watching our 9-year-old son play!

**Olivia:** I thought he promised that he wouldn't bet anymore? He's gotten you into such a hole financially. I can't believe he would do that again!

**Phoebe:** I'm on the computer right now looking at our bank account. He got paid on Friday, and that money was deposited. On Saturday, it looks like he withdrew money four different times to two different sports betting apps. On Sunday, he had three more withdrawals to PayPal and Venmo. I can't even breathe right now. I feel nauseous. My heart is pounding. I can't think, and I don't know what to do.

**Olivia:** He has done this to your family so many times Phoebe!

**Phoebe:** I know. I hate him so much right now. I really thought the last time he did this would be the last time. Remember how much trouble we got in? I had to beg family for money and then went to different charities to ask for financial help. It was so embarrassing! You know he doesn't like me to ask for help. He was mad because what he really wanted to do was take the money we were getting from family and charity and *use it to gamble!* He said that if I was smart, I'd let him use that money to make more money. Then we could pay off what we owe and even have a little extra. He said it was *my* fault that we were in the hole. How do you even deal with that level of insanity?

**Olivia:** What are you going to do?

**Phoebe:** I don't know.

**Olivia:** Could you go to family again for money?

**Phoebe:** I don't think so. You know my family doesn't have much to give! They would help if I asked but they don't have extra. Remember my dad came over last time and put gas in my car and my mom kept making casseroles for us? They would do anything to help but my dad believes that Jack should be the one taking care of us. My parents are wonderful. I always thought I would marry someone and have that same kind of love. The kind of love where family matters more than anything. Jack cares more about the big win. And now we don't have money to pay our rent. AGAIN! I haven't even bought groceries for the week. I'd like to pack our bags and leave, but then I'd worry about him and who is going to take care of him. He can't even do dishes. He's so good with the kids. Loving and fun. They love him so much and have no idea what is happening with his gambling. And I don't want them to know. They think he is a fun dad!

**Olivia:** Well, he really is a fun dad and plays with them. It's just that fun dad doesn't mean responsible dad.

**Phoebe**: We don't even have *groceries*, Ol.

**Olivia:** Phoebe, I think you really need help. I would be more than happy to help you financially, but then my money would end up going down the Jack Gambling Drain. I love you and I'd help you, but everything that goes to you ends up in his hands and he's not taking care of you and the family financially.

**Phoebe:** I know. I know you're totally right. He can't be trusted with money. I have to pay all the bills because he would put off paying them. If I didn't pay them, I'm not sure any of them would be paid!

**Olivia:** Have you thought about getting help?

**Phoebe**: He needs help, but he won't go.

**Olivia:** I'm talking about YOU getting help. Obviously, he needs help, but I'm more worried about you right now. I feel like you need help on an emotional level because this has been taking a toll on your physical and mental health. You've told me before that you haven't been sleeping well and that you feel depressed and anxious ever since he started gambling. I'm worried about YOU. It's not like you to be depressed and worried like this. You're not the same light-hearted, fun Pheebs. I know you're trying to protect your children and are hiding this from them, but they are smart Phoebe. They know something is wrong. Just the other day, Carlie said she wanted to ask for a bike so she could learn to ride but she didn't want to stress you out by asking you to spend any money.

**Phoebe (crying):** Ollie, I don't know what to do.

**Olivia:** Have you thought about getting help?

**Phoebe:** As in a financial counselor?

**Olivia:** Yes, okay. And also, mental health counseling?

**Phoebe:** I wouldn't mind talking to a counselor, but I can't! I don't have the time or the money to go to counseling!

**Olivia:** Well, let's focus on facts here. You want to get help and talk to a counselor but time and money are preventing you from going?

**Phoebe:** Yes, especially money. I can't even buy groceries right now.

**Olivia:** Okay. You don't have money for rent and food today. Seems like the facts that you have told me are that:

1. Jack gambled his paycheck.
2. Your rent check bounced.
3. He's done this before and promised to not do it again.
4. He did it again.
5. You are upset and don't know what to do.
6. You can't buy groceries for you and your children.
7. In the past when he did this, you borrowed from family and charities.
8. You are not sure if you can do that again because your parents don't have extra to give.
9. You have to pay the bills each month because he won't.
10. You are not sleeping well and have been depressed and anxious about this.

Did I miss anything?

**Phoebe:** Well, that list is pretty devastating to hear.

**Olivia:** Okay, well let's add to it. You are working. You have a job. You have me. Your children are wonderful. At your work, do you have an Employee Assistance Program with counselors available?

**Phoebe:** Oh. I didn't even think of that. I'm not sure.

**Olivia:** Okay. Something to look into to see if it's available to you. There are also programs for people who gamble and their families. I believe they might be free and online. Have you looked into any of those?

**Phoebe:** No, but that's not a bad idea.

**Olivia:** Okay, what would be the pros of seeking help? What would be the cons?

**Phoebe:** Well, the pros would be that I could talk to a professional about ways to protect myself. I could learn how to put up boundaries so he can't do this to me anymore. Cons would be that he would be mad at me. And that it's embarrassing to tell someone the situation we are in.

**Olivia:** Okay. Sounds like a good place to start maybe. Just think about whether or not it's worth it to investigate options for free counseling and support for the situation you are in. This is really bad Phoebe and it's so hard to watch you suffer.

**Phoebe:** I know. I think you're right. I just looked up resources for gambling and found a National Hotline for people who gamble and their family members to call. It's definitely worth a shot to see if we can get some help.

**Olivia:** Would you be willing to call now?

**Phoebe:** I'm calling right now. Love you.

**Olivia:** Love you too, Pheebs.

## AN ANALYSIS OF PHOEBE'S STORY

Phoebe's husband has an addiction to gambling. His gambling has caused financial strain on the family and Phoebe is at her wit's end. She calls her best friend in exasperation. Her friend asks Phoebe about getting help. Phoebe indicates that she has no time or money for help, insisting she doesn't even have grocery money for the week. Her friend helps her to consider some free or low-cost services, such as her employee assistance program or online support groups.

Upon realizing that she might have a couple of options for help, she decides it would be good to get help establishing boundaries between her and her husband so that he can't hurt the family financially.

Phoebe's initial thoughts/feelings about treatment were:

| |
|---|
| **INITIAL THOUGHTS** |
| "I don't have time." |
| "I don't have money." |
| **INITIAL FEELINGS** |
| Overwhelmed, angry, scared |
| **INITIAL BEHAVIORS** |
| Protecting husband |
| Finding money to pay bills |
| During the discussion with Olivia, she reconsiders her thoughts on seeking help: |
| **NEW THOUGHTS** |
| "I have time right now for a call." |
| "I don't have money but there might be some free resources available to me." |
| **NEW FEELINGS** |
| Curious |
| Hopeful |
| **NEW BEHAVIORS** |
| Call National Hotline for people with gambling problems. |
| Investigate whether she has counseling available through her work. |

# WORKING THROUGH
# RESISTANCE TO TREATMENT

Some people indicate that the reason they will not go to treatment is because they do not have the time or the money for treatment. Typically, this is not *the* reason an individual is refusing treatment, but instead one used to end a discussion regarding treatment. It might be true that they have little time or few resources; however, it's typically not the real reason why someone hesitates to go. When someone says that they don't have the time or money for treatment, there are ways to have a discussion with them on this belief.

The next section of this chapter will focus on how to have conversations with individuals who indicate that they do not have time and/or money for mental health or substance use treatment; and ways you can help someone reconsider these thoughts so they are more likely to consider getting help.

Someone who believes that they don't have time or money will say things like:

- "I don't have time for that."
- "I don't have the money for that."
- "I'm too busy just trying to survive."

If someone in your life is refusing treatment and saying these thoughts, there are a variety of ways to have a discussion with them to get them to reconsider these thoughts.

These include:

1.  Assess the facts.

2.  Conduct a cost/benefit analysis.

## ASSESS THE FACTS

Time and money are tricky. I've worked with individuals on both ends of the continuum with respect to time and money and everyone says similar things. "I don't have time." "I don't have money."

It's important to understand what a person is really saying when they report they don't have time or money for something. **It's possible, even likely, that they are stating that they do not wish to use their time and/or money for (insert anything).** The truth is that even among people who are exceptionally busy or highly under-resourced, **people are amazingly able to do the things that they want to do.**

There are two important steps to consider when talking with someone who says that they don't have the time or the money:

1.  Get the facts about time/money.

2.  Get the facts about whether they have interest in and barriers to treatment.

Remember to:

*   Let them know that you care about them. The conversation is coming from a place of love and care.

*   Resist the urge to criticize or judge.

- Understand how denial might be playing a role in the discussion.
- Stay calm. If either of you becomes angry or agitated, it's best to walk away and try again another day/time.
- Set healthy boundaries.

| DO'S | DON'TS |
|---|---|
| • Acknowledge and validate how busy they are<br>• Acknowledge and validate financial barriers<br>• Acknowledge and validate distress<br>• Inquire about availability of time (1 hour per week)<br>• Ask about options (including online, free options) | • Let the discussion end here<br><br>• Let distress end the discussion |

Things to consider include:

- For individuals with financial barriers and need, there are free, online resources available for most conditions (see Chapter 11).
- For individuals with time barriers, most treatment options require one hour per week (or less).

# ASSESSING THE FACTS ABOUT TIME AND/OR MONEY

Take time to list out the facts. These could be things like:

1. Identify the problem behavior (drugs/alcohol, gambling, overeating, oversleeping, avoiding, isolating, overspending, aggression, etc.).

2. Track the amount of time spent engaging in problem behavior.

3. Track amount of money spent engaging in problem behavior.

4. Identify consequences of engaging in problem behavior (lost productivity, relationship difficulties, poor health, etc.).

5. Assess level of interest in changing problem behavior. For example, this could be something like on a scale of 1-10, how much do I want to change this particular behavior?

6. Identify any barriers to changing the behavior (people in life that reinforce the behavior such as a drinker living with people who have alcohol around the house).

7. Identify whether there are any barriers that could be removed (such as removing alcohol from the house).

8. Evaluate the facts and assess the big picture.

# THE ROLE OF DENIAL

Denial is a cognitive distortion (thinking style) or defense mechanism that helps people cope with negative emotions/stress. It's easier to believe that you don't really have a problem than to acknowledge that you might. It can be challenging to list facts regarding a problem behavior if the individual in question denies the problem exists. This is when it can be important to understand how our brains lie.

Humans have an amazing capacity to lie. We lie to ourselves. Often. Some of these lies are necessary for survival (For example, telling yourself that you're totally fine with waking up every 2 hours to feed a newborn baby. It's fine. It's totally fine). Other lies are more catastrophic (I need another drink even though my blood alcohol content is at its limit). Whether the lies are protective or destructive, it's a good idea to be aware of our lies.

An example of how lies interfere with functioning is how some of us act when we are sick. Getting sick is inconvenient, uncomfortable and annoying. You can't be sick if you have to be productive at work, have a family to take care of and errands to run. Someone getting sick might say, "I'm okay. It's not that bad." They could be resting and protecting others from getting sick, but instead they run around and function as though germy little bugs aren't running rampant through their immune system. It might take a good 24–48 hours of feeling bad before they admit they don't feel good. Meanwhile, those same people on other occasions have thought, "Man, I wish I could get sick for a couple of days just so I can rest for a minute and catch up on my sleep. I'd love a couple of sick days." This is the conundrum of the human condition. We want what we want until we have it, and then we don't want it or can't enjoy it. And the whole time, we feed ourselves lies.

**We are only as sick as our secrets.** This is a common sentence heard in addiction treatment. And it's a useful one to consider. Below are some scenarios and examples of lies told that result in continued problem behavior and/or suffering:

## GAMBLING

The "gambler's fallacy" is the belief that you can predict the outcome based on prior results; therefore, there is an illusion of control over the situation. The belief is that you can influence the outcome through skill/strategy.

Lies people who gamble tell themselves include:

- "I'm going to win."

- "If you would just support me, I could win big for our family."

- "I don't do it all the time, so it's not a problem."

- "It's my money. I can do whatever I want with it."

- "I can stop whenever I want."

- "I'll pay back whatever I owe as soon as I win big."

- "I'm not hurting anyone."

- "I just had bad luck today."

## SUBSTANCES

Any statement that someone with a drug or alcohol problem tells them to drink or use is a lie.

Lies people with substance use disorders tell themselves include:

- "It's only one (or a little bit)."
- "Just this one time."
- "It's a big event/holiday/occasion/dinner/celebration/game, so I'll only do it because of the occasion."
- "I didn't have any yesterday, so I'm okay to drink/use now."
- "I'm really stressed, and I need it to calm me down."
- "I'm really angry so I need to drink/use."
- "At least it's not hard alcohol, one beer won't hurt."
- "At least it's not that drug, this other drug isn't as bad."
- "I can stop whenever I want."
- "I'm not hurting anyone."

Listing out the facts, and assessing interest in, barriers to, and lies told about, the problem behavior is a useful exercise when considering whether someone has time/money to engage in treatment. It helps outline the BIG PICTURE of the situation, which can get blurry when inside of it.

# CALCULATE COSTS/BENEFITS OF TREATMENT

While it is useful to outline the facts regarding a problem behavior, it can also be useful to identify pros and cons of seeking treatment. Sit down and make a list of any and all the pros and cons you can think of for seeking treatment for a specific condition. Once you have this information, it may be easier to objectively and honestly consider treatment as an option.

Ultimately, the individual in need has the option to make a choice for themselves. A list of pros/cons can be helpful for this decision. It's important to be as honest as possible when creating this list. In other words, don't just report the cons if you don't want to consider treatment. Honestly consider the pros as well.

Consider the following example of a pro/con list for someone considering treatment for alcohol use:

**Pros**

- Learn strategies to reduce alcohol use
- Identify coping skills other than alcohol
- Identify triggers for drinking alcohol
- Learn how to regulate negative emotions without alcohol
- Improve sleep

**Cons**

- Discomfort when reducing alcohol use
- Discomfort talking about feelings

- Discomfort considering that you might have a problem with alcohol

Here's another example, a pro/con list for someone considering treatment for a gambling problem. Gambling disorder is an uncontrollable urge to keep gambling despite problems it causes in your life (financial, relationship, health, legal). Consequences of a gambling disorder can be devastating.

**Pros**

- Learn strategies to reduce gambling
- Identify ways to cope with discomfort
- Identify triggers for gambling
- Save money that would be spent on gambling
- Understand thoughts/feelings related to gambling
- Identify risks of continued gambling (debt/bankruptcy, loss of family, housing insecurity, legal issues, work issues, health issues such as depression, anxiety, substance use disorders, heart attacks, high blood pressure, headaches)
- Learn how to say no (to gambling and to lying about gambling)

**Cons**

- Identify as someone with a gambling problem
- Discomfort of saying no to gambling (irritable, restless, bored, pre-occupied with thoughts about gambling, difficulty concentrating)

Just like with assessing the facts, assessing the pros and cons of seeking treatment helps outline the big picture. The big picture can be difficult to see when inside of the situation.

# KEY SUMMARY POINTS

The main idea of this chapter is that people don't seek help because they believe they don't have the time or the money for treatment.

Strategies to overcome these thoughts include:

- Assess the facts
- Calculate costs/benefits of treatment

## DECISION TREE

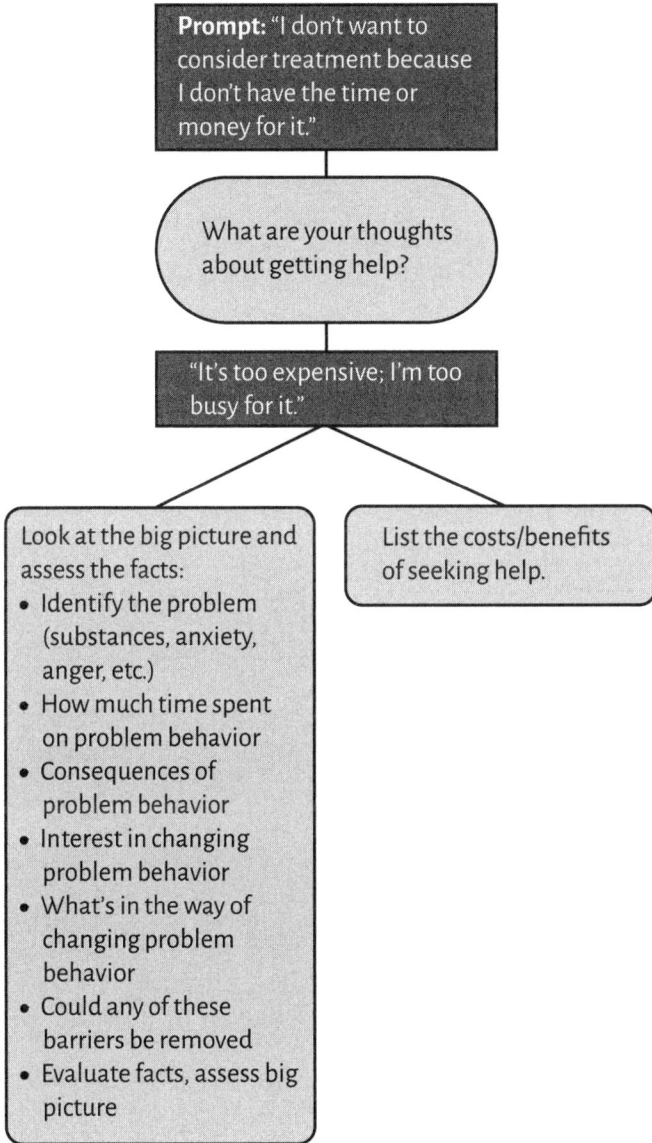

**Prompt:** "I don't want to consider treatment because I don't have the time or money for it."

What are your thoughts about getting help?

"It's too expensive; I'm too busy for it."

Look at the big picture and assess the facts:
- Identify the problem (substances, anxiety, anger, etc.)
- How much time spent on problem behavior
- Consequences of problem behavior
- Interest in changing problem behavior
- What's in the way of changing problem behavior
- Could any of these barriers be removed
- Evaluate facts, assess big picture

List the costs/benefits of seeking help.

# CHAPTER 11

# TALKING TO LOVED ONES

**T**HE GOAL OF these discussions is to talk about getting help for a mental health or substance use disorder. Allow yourself time to understand their thoughts about getting help and ask to discuss it further. Helping someone change their thoughts about seeking help can change their likelihood of getting help.

Remember the four basic communication skills discussed in Chapter 1. Without these, discussions are likely to be ineffective and unproductive. There is no point in talking if you are unable to meet your goals. To meet your goal of having someone consider treatment, it's important to be empathic, genuine, respectful and a good listener. This allows the other person to truly invest in the discussion. This is also true when you are talking to yourself about treatment (or anything)!

- Empathy is the ability to see someone else's perspective.

- Genuineness is being your true self and authentic.

- Positive regard is the capacity to be respectful.

- Active listening involves hearing what someone says, taking time to understand what they say and responding to them to ensure that what you heard was what they communicated.

# COMPLICATING FACTORS

There are circumstances that make conversations about seeking help difficult. These include cognitive impairment, enabling, strong emotions, and manipulation.

## COGNITIVE IMPAIRMENT

Cognitive impairment can make discussions about treatment utilization difficult. Cognitive impairment is when someone has problems thinking, learning, and making decisions. Cognitive impairment can stem from a variety of conditions including autism spectrum disorders, dementia, psychosis, traumatic brain injury, substance use, and some physical conditions. If you know or suspect someone has cognitive impairment, please consult with a specialist for further guidance. If the impairment is temporary, such as when someone is intoxicated, wait to talk with them when they are no longer impaired.

## ENABLING

Enabling is not a healthy behavior. Engaging in enabling prolongs poor functioning. **While the intention may be to minimize suffering, enabling increases poor decisions and extends suffering.** It is ironic that many people who enable want to help their loved ones be comfortable and avoid bad outcomes; however, by enabling, they actually become a part of the dysfunction. This is one of the reasons why it can be difficult to stop. If you are constantly trying to protect someone from a bad situation, it's time to take a step back, see the big picture, and reassess facts. It is important that people who enable recognize their role in the situation and seek help to learn to set healthy boundaries and learn how and when to use the word no.

Consider the following examples of enabling:

- **Your child is frustrated with math homework, so you do it for them.** If you continue to do their math homework for them, they will never learn the concepts they are supposed to learn. You are doing the work for them instead of creating opportunities for them to learn ways to manage their stress about math. You are also interfering with their ability to learn math.

- **Your spouse has anxiety.** When they feel anxious, they avoid whatever is causing them to feel anxious. Instead of supporting their learning to face anxious feelings you support their avoidance of the source of anxiety. An example of this is when someone gets anxious about going to the dentist. Instead of helping them learn ways to manage their anxiety, you support their avoidance of the dentist. The anxiety goes away temporarily. They don't learn how to manage anxious feelings. Avoidance becomes reinforced. Avoidance becomes their "treatment"; and you become part of their treatment center. They are also unlikely to seek help for their anxiety. Regular dental care is important but what would happen in this scenario is a dental emergency. Someone avoiding dental treatment due to anxiety could have catastrophic consequences.

- **Someone has a drug addiction and does not have a job or home.** They have difficulty finding money to pay for their drugs. You provide them with food and housing and give them money to pay for drugs. You justify this by telling yourself, "At least they are off the street and safe." Reality is that you are paying them to use drugs and making it easier for them to continue to use.

Notice in all of these examples, the person who enables is attempting to help their loved one avoid discomfort. Discomfort is not the enemy. It's a part of life and learning to manage it is critical to a healthy lifestyle. Learning how to manage discomfort and feelings of anxiety are an important part of life and should not be sidestepped. The "treatment" the person who enables provides is not helping. It is unlikely that someone will seek professional help when a person who enables is actively involved.

## STRONG EMOTIONS

It's possible that discussions on help-seeking become emotional. Consider when the discussion becomes so emotional that it is unproductive. There is a fine line determining the stopping point because of agitation or fear. Agitation and fear, in and of themselves, are okay. The point where someone is no longer capable of rational discussion is the point where discussions should end. This may be when someone starts yelling or becomes unable to focus on the discussion at hand.

Techniques to de-escalate strong emotions include:

- Maintain a calm, relaxed presence with an open mind (eye contact, non-threatening body posture).

- Speak with a calm, even tone of voice.

- Engage in active listening. By engaging in active listening, you're not asking question after question, but instead hearing what they are trying to communicate and ensuring that you heard them correctly. This helps someone feel heard and validated. It does not mean that you agree with what they are saying, but that you are willing to hear their thoughts.

- Don't interrupt.

- Avoid making accusations, judgments, criticisms.

- Discuss options of how to have the conversation. (Where, when, with whom, stopping points, etc.)

It's also possible that you are the one that has strong emotions or becomes agitated. It's very difficult to have a rational conversation with someone who engages in unhealthy behavior when their behavior harms you. This is especially hard if they have no desire to change their unhealthy behavior. It can leave you feeling helpless and in despair.

Options to consider if you feel you are unable to continue the discussion include:

- Inviting a third party to lead the discussion.

- Taking a time out and coming back to the discussion the next day.

- Seeking professional help.

## MANIPULATION

Similar to strong emotions, manipulation can come into play. Manipulation is a harmful behavior some people use to control others to achieve a goal. Examples include the silent treatment, guilt trips, isolation, throwing tantrums, and triangulation (among others). Manipulation has no role in healthy relationships or in healthy communication. If you are dealing with someone who is manipulative, boundaries are essential.

| TIPS TO IMPROVE DISCUSSIONS | |
| --- | --- |
| **EMPATHY** | Understand the situation from their perspective. |
| **GENUINE** | Be your true self in the discussion. |
| **RESPECT** | Value yourself and your loved one. |
| **ACTIVE LISTENING** | Essential for healthy communication: 1. *Hear* their words. 2. *Understand* what you hear. 3. *State back* what you heard to confirm understanding. |
| **EMOTIONS** | Stay calm and keep an open mind during these discussions. Strong emotions such as anger and fear make discussions difficult. Take time out to calm down high emotions. Practice de-escalation skills. |
| **FEELING STUCK** | Consider the reason for being stuck. If movement forward is possible, ask to continue discussion. If movement forward is unlikely, please seek professional help. |

| TIMING | Identify who should be participating in the discussion. |
|---|---|
| | Ensure no one is impaired/intoxicated. |
| | Being sleep deprived can make discussions more emotional, be aware of making sure that you are rested and have good nutrition. |
| | Consider when someone is capable of having productive discussion (don't surprise them or wait until they are hungry and tired to start the discussion). |
| **JUDGEMENT/ OPINIONS** | Be neutral, calm, and keep an open mind. |
| | Remember this is ultimately their decision. |
| **DISCUSSION LEADER** | Determine who is best to lead discussion with loved one. |
| **EMOTIONAL MANIPULATION** | If dealing with a loved one who is manipulative, consider inviting a professional third person to lead the discussion. |

# FINAL WORDS

"Do not judge me by my successes, judge me by how many times I fell down and got back up."

—NELSON MANDELA

HUMANS ARE MADE up of stories.

We can *change* our story.

This book represents years of working with people in pain who refused to get help. The human spirit has amazing capacity when it comes to carrying pain. We adapt to it, sit in it, and sometimes even have difficulty letting it go. The pain can become who you are, a burden, or even a friend. Allowing me to walk with you, even while you're in pain, has been an honor. I'm in awe of the strength and joy I've seen watching some of you push through.

While we have an incredible capacity to endure pain, we also have a profound ability to overcome. Even when we think we can't endure, we do. Pain is an opportunity to learn more, try something new, see the world from a different perspective, live, breathe, be, and try again. Be willing to step outside the pain, to be free from it, to walk with it differently. There is no option for a pain-free life. To live means to experience pain. We all lose and hurt and win and triumph occasionally. And the grace with which you walk through these experiences can make such a difference.

Life is so hard. Why be anything but kind?

# ABOUT THE AUTHOR

**Tracy Stecker, PhD**, is a psychologist at the Medical University of South Carolina and at the Center of Excellence for Suicide Prevention in the Department of Veterans Affairs. Dr. Stecker's work focuses on help-seeking behavior among individuals with mental health and substance use concerns. Her work has been nationally recognized, including by the Presidential Task Force PREVENTS in 2020. She has been funded by the National Institute of Mental Health, the National Institute of Alcoholism and Alcohol Abuse, the National Institute of Drug Abuse, the Department of Defense, and the Department of Veterans Affairs to develop and test cognitive-behavioral interventions to increase treatment seeking among individuals with symptoms of PTSD, substance use, and suicidality. She is widely published in scientific journals and is the author of two books, including a book on PTSD survival stories.

# ACKNOWLEDGEMENTS

I've been writing this book my whole life, in some ways, so there are quite a few people to thank.

Thank you to Hatherleigh Press (Ryan Tumambing and Ryan Kennedy) for taking a chance on this book.

I'm grateful for my time at the University of California San Francisco, where I completed a fellowship with Dr. Henry Kahn and launched a career focused on helping those in need to seek help.

Thank you to Dr. John Fortney, who tried his damnedest to teach me how to write (and rewrite).

I'm grateful for my time at Dartmouth College. To Dr. Bob Drake for shining a light on humanity, even in an academic setting. Very special thanks to Katrina Whyman, Elizabeth Belbruno, and Nicholas Streltzov. You three are awe-inspiring and magical people and I will never forget our work together.

There are multiple colleagues to thank. I am particularly grateful to Dr. Charles Hoge, Dr. Kyle Possemato, Dr. Ken Conner, Dr. Steve Maisto, Dr. Sudie Back, Dr. Delisa Brown, Dr. Teresa Kelechi, Sarah Szafranski, Tyler Webb, Dr. Caitlin Titus. And to Dr. Ron Acierno who time and time again will stand up and fight for what is right.

I don't even know how to thank these next two people. I imagine when it's time to look back on my career, I'll see a lot of Lee and Nik. I am proud and honored to work with you two. LINKTS.

To my friends for laughing it out with me. Deepest gratitude to Becky Horvath and Amanda Pendley. Thank you for being there every step of the way.

For all of those who trusted me with their pain, may you have mercy and healing.

Years ago, I was with my youngest in the baby pool portion of a pool area when a baby fell into the pool. The ten or so mothers sitting right there squealed, and I squealed along with them. Another mother further away ran over and grabbed the baby from under the water. Most of us went into a state of shock versus action. Thankfully, that one mother acted to rescue the baby quickly. She reminded me of the veterans I work with. I asked her if she had served in the United States military. She had. To those who served, and who put their lives on the line to serve God and country, thank you. To all those who help, thank you.

The characters portrayed within are fictitious. Even so, I drew inspiration from several amazing people including Tory Gentges, Wayne Pendley, Syd Lorandeau, and Tyler Webb.

Samantha Nicole. You are stronger than you know. Smarter than you think. And taught me more than you can imagine.

My dear Gregory. Thank you for giving me time to breathe. And for everything.

# RESOURCES

## NATIONAL ORGANIZATIONS

National Institute of Health

National Institute for Mental Health (NIMH)

National Institute for Drug Abuse (NIDA)

National Institute for Alcohol Abuse and Alcoholism (NIAAA)

National Center for Complementary and Integrative Medicine (NCCIH)

## RESOURCES FOR PAIN MANAGEMENT

va.gov/painmanagement

va.gov/wholehealth

iasp-pain.org/resources

## RESOURCES FOR TREATMENT AND INFORMATION ABOUT MENTAL HEALTH AND SUBSTANCE USE

mentalhealth.va.gov

mentalhealth.va.gov/substance-use/index.asp

cdc.gov/mental-health

findtreatment.samhsa.gov

refugerecovery.org

na.org (Narcotics Anonymous)

psychologytoday.com/us/therapists

samhsa.gov/find-help/national-helpline

recoverydharma.online

betterhelp.com

asam.org

niaaa.nih.gov

nami.org (National Alliance on Mental Illness)

## FREE AND CONFIDENTIAL SUPPORT LINES FOR DISTRESS, CRISIS AND INFORMATION

### Veterans Crisis Line

Call toll-free number 1-800-273-TALK, Press 1

Text 838255.

Chat online at www.veteranscrisisline.net/get-help-now/chat/

You'll be immediately connected to suicide prevention and mental health professionals.

### SAMHSA National Helpline

Call 1-800-662-HELP (4357)

This provides 24-hour free and confidential treatment referral and information about mental and/or substance use disorders, prevention, and recovery.

Other options are to go to the nearest hospital emergency department and/or call 911.